Communicating in Professions and Organizations

Series Editor
Jonathan Crichton
University of South Australia
Adelaide, SA, Australia

This ground-breaking series is edited by Jonathan Crichton, Senior Lecturer in Applied Linguistics at the University of South Australia. It provides a venue for research on issues of language and communication that matter to professionals, their clients and stakeholders. Books in the series explore the relevance and real world impact of communication research in professional practice and forge reciprocal links between researchers in applied linguistics/discourse analysis and practitioners from numerous professions, including healthcare, education, business and trade, law, media, science and technology.

Central to this agenda, the series responds to contemporary challenges to professional practice that are bringing issues of language and communication to the fore. These include:

- The growing importance of communication as a form of professional expertise that needs to be made visible and developed as a resource for professionals
- Political, economic, technological and social changes that are transforming communicative practices in professions and organisations
- Increasing mobility and diversity (geographical, technological, cultural, linguistic) of organisations, professionals and clients

Books in the series combine up to date overviews of issues of language and communication relevant to the particular professional domain with original research that addresses these issues at relevant sites. The authors also explore the practical implications of this research for the professions/organisations in question.

We are actively commissioning projects for this series and welcome proposals from authors whose experience combines linguistic and professional expertise, from those who have long-standing knowledge of the professional and organisational settings in which their books are located and joint editing/authorship by language researchers and professional practitioners.

The series is designed for both academic and professional readers, for scholars and students in Applied Linguistics, Communication Studies and related fields, and for members of the professions and organisations whose practice is the focus of the series.

More information about this series at
http://www.palgrave.com/gp/series/14904

Geert Jacobs • Sofie Decock
Editors

Good Data in Business and Professional Discourse Research and Teaching

Further Explorations

palgrave
macmillan

Editors
Geert Jacobs
Department of Linguistics
Ghent University
Ghent, Belgium

Sofie Decock
Department of Translation, Interpreting
and Communication
Ghent University
Ghent, Belgium

Communicating in Professions and Organizations
ISBN 978-3-030-61756-1 ISBN 978-3-030-61757-8 (eBook)
https://doi.org/10.1007/978-3-030-61757-8

Cover illustration: Christian Wagner / Alamy Stock Photo

This Palgrave Macmillan imprint is published by the registered company Springer Nature Switzerland AG.
The registered company address is: Gewerbestrasse 11, 6330 Cham, Switzerland

Praise for *Good Data in Business and Professional Discourse Research and Teaching*

"This collection expertly balances interdisciplinary approaches, hands-on fieldwork, and academic rigour. The contributors team up to provide an ambitious and engaging, multifaceted exploration of the role of data in business and professional communication. This collection nicely advances common ground between researchers and practitioners and will provide authoritative insights for all interested in the role of language and communication in business or professional settings."

—Glen Michael Alessi, *University of Modena and Reggio Emilia, Italy*

"A timely, ground-breaking volume relying on a fundamental question—"What counts as data?"—as the focus for a broad-based study of business and professional discourse. The result is an enhanced understanding of the importance of organizational contexts in multilingual environments, which requires an expansion of data collection and analysis beyond traditional boundaries and demonstrates innovative uses of qualitative research."

—James M. Dubinsky, *Rhetoric & Writing, Virginia Tech, Past President & Executive Director, Association for Business Communication (ABC)*

Contents

Notes on Contributors

Deborah C. Andrews is Professor of English, Emerita, and former director of the Center for Material Culture Studies at the University of Delaware, USA. She has published several articles, book chapters, and textbooks on business, professional and technical communication, especially in the international community.

Fanny Domenec is a Senior Lecturer at Paris 2 University. She teaches English for economics and finance. Her research work focuses on corporate discourse and culture in contexts of crisis. She also works on evolutions linked to ethics in the professional world (new discursive genres, professions or legal structures).

Janet Holmes is Emeritus Professor of Linguistics and Associate Director of the Wellington Language in the Workplace project. She researches in the area of sociolinguistics, specialising in workplace discourse and language and gender. With the Language in the Workplace team, she is currently investigating workplace discourse of relevance to migrants.

Philippe Millot is a Senior Lecturer in English for Specific Purposes at the University of Lyon (Jean Moulin, Lyon 3). His research interests include ESP, specialised domains and corpus linguistics. His research more particularly focuses on business and professional discourse analysis. He is also the associate editor of *ASp*, the French journal of ESP.

Sofie Decock is Associate Professor at the Department of Translation, Interpreting and Communication at Ghent University, Belgium. She conducts research in the fields of business communication and German Studies with a focus on discourse, (intercultural, digital) interactions and persuasion.

Christina Efthymiadou is a Lecturer in International Management at Bristol Business School. She holds a PhD in Intercultural Communication from the University of Warwick and her main research interests include the construction and negotiation of identity, professional discourse and culture. Christina adopts ethnographic methods and works mainly with interactional data.

Geert Jacobs is a Professor of English for Specific Purposes and Business Discourse at the Department of Linguistics at Ghent University. He has researched wide-ranging forms of institutional interaction and of news text and talk.

Hiromasa Tanaka Ed. D is a Professor at International Studies Department, School of Humanities, Meisei University, Japan. He teaches research methodology courses for graduate students, and project-based courses for undergraduate students. As a consultant, Hiromasa has been involved a number of human resource development system design for business corporations.

Astrid Vandendaele is an Assistant Professor of Journalism and New Media at Leiden University. Her research focuses on news production processes as well as communication processes in an institutional context from a linguistic ethnographic perspective. She teaches courses in Journalism and New Media at Leiden University as well as Business and Scientific Communication at Ghent University.

Bernadette Vine is Senior Researcher and Corpus Manager for the Wellington Language in the Workplace Project (www.victoria.ac.nz/lwp/). Bernadette's research interests include workplace communication, leadership and New Zealand English. Her publications include her recent textbook, *Introducing Language in the Workplace* (Cambridge University Press, 2020).

List of Figures

List of Tables

1

What Counts as Good Data in Business and Professional Discourse Research and Training?

Sofie Decock and Geert Jacobs

In *The Ins and Outs of Business and Professional Discourse Research* Alessi and Jacobs (2016) brought together a number of studies that characterize the field of business and professional discourse as essentially contextual and intertextual, but also as reflexive and self-critical. They indicated that many of those active in the field seemed to be struggling towards reconciling the prescriptive ambitions of a US-centred business communication tradition with a more descriptive approach favoured in discourse studies and applied linguistics elsewhere. The "Ins and Outs" volume was focused on two key stages of the research process: the initial stage of negotiating access, collecting data, designing/refining a research question and deciding

S. Decock (✉)
Department of Translation, Interpreting and Communication,
Ghent University, Ghent, Belgium
e-mail: sofie.decock@ugent.be

G. Jacobs
Department of Linguistics, Ghent University, Ghent, Belgium
e-mail: geert.jacobs@ugent.be

G. Jacobs, S. Decock (eds.), *Good Data in Business and Professional Discourse Research and Teaching*, Communicating in Professions and Organizations,
https://doi.org/10.1007/978-3-030-61757-8_1

on a methodology (the so-called 'Ins') and the very final step of wrapping up the research by feeding the research results back to the world of practitioners and considering real-world applications (the 'Outs'). The current collection of chapters follows up on this by concentrating on a specific aspect of the 'Ins' stage and engaging with a key question that could be phrased rather informally as: what counts as good data for business and professional discourse research and training? The reason for doing so is that throughout the various contributions to the original Ins and Outs volume there seemed to be a number of implicit assumptions about what kind of data should be studied and about how they should be analysed. It is these underlying assumptions that the present collection aims to go into more deeply. In particular, the following four issues are focused on:

(1) authenticity: a substantial part of the study of business and professional discourse has been haunted by a mantra to look at authentic, i.e. "actual", communicative practices. But why is this? And what makes practices actual? What are actual, or authentic, data, to begin with? And what are second-hand data? Does authenticity impact on the potential for applying the results of our work in the real world? Can authenticity be simulated?

It should be noted here that authenticity is not a straightforward concept (see, for example, Van Leeuwen (2001) for an interesting reflection on its many dimensions, including authorship, accuracy and truth). Rather than starting out from a simple definition, in this chapter we propose a close reading of the chapters in this volume to explore how the term has been variously used in business and professional discourse research and training.

(2) triangulation: a lot of business and professional discourse research aspires towards triangulation. While triangulation is most commonly associated with the idea of using different methods in order to validate or enrich research results, there is no single, widely accepted definition of it. In spite of this lack of clarity, why has triangulation been so popular in the field? And what challenges does it entail? What are the criteria for a sound mixed-methods approach?

Like for authenticity we will explore in this chapter how the term triangulation is used, referring to data sampling and methodological combinations (mixed methods) as well as theoretical variety.

(3) background: as the study of business and professional discourse is seen as essentially contextual, it is generally agreed that there is a strong need for understanding what is actually going on in the data at hand. For lack of a better term we propose 'background' here, to refer to the rich, multifaceted and often elusive world that the practitioners we investigate inhabit. But how can we reach this understanding and bridge the gap between scholars and practitioners? How familiar do we, as analysts, have to be with the data that we are studying? Can an interdisciplinary approach be beneficial in trying to bridge the gap?

(4) relevance: there has been a long-standing discussion in management studies about whether scholars are sufficiently considering the practical relevance of their research, suggesting that many of them are merely pursuing scientific rigour instead (Hodgkinson and Rousseau 2009; Kieser and Leiner 2009; Wolf and Rosenberg 2012). Some of the questions that can be raised here include: how can rigour and relevance be reconciled? Is there a conflict between the two in the first place? Or, instead, does one require the other?

Relevance is a key concept in that it connects business and professional discourse research with business and professional discourse training by zooming in on how the analysis of a mix of authentic data, along with the backgrounds they are part of, can be used as input ('applied', some would say) to a range of types of training resources.

In line with the 2016 Ins and Outs volume, we believe that the questions listed above are especially relevant in a field that, by its very nature, has been richly interdisciplinary, attracting scholars from applied linguistics and discourse studies as well as sociology, communication science, management, marketing and information systems and that has traditionally been looking to connect scholarship with classroom teaching and pedagogy as well as with consultancy and practice.

In this introduction, rather than presenting the traditional bird's eye view of what has previously been written on the topic of this volume followed by the standard summaries of the various chapters in it, we propose what could be seen as a meta-analysis of how the four issues spelled out above are dealt with in the wide-ranging empirical work that is included here. The reason why we do not opt for the former is that the issues, as far as we know, have never been treated systematically and consistently in a single study, at least not in the field of business and professional discourse research. Relevant discussions are scattered across the literature, often hidden in methodological sections or even footnotes. Hence, presenting a bird's eye view of the relevant literature is bound to be selective and idiosyncratic, a matter of luck and serendipity rather than sustained scrutiny. The meta-analysis we propose instead is meant to bring into the light some of the assumptions and ambitions on what are good data that underlie the research presented here. It is not aimed at exhaustive or systematic coverage of the four issues listed above (nor at a detailed rendering of what the chapters are about, for that matter) and it will, no surprise, reveal internal inconsistencies and conflicts between the chapters. Instead, we hope that it is precisely in its incompleteness and uncertainty that lies a good basis for initiating the kind of systematic reflection on theoretical underpinnings that mark all mature academic disciplines.

Authenticity

That the study of business and professional discourse is deeply concerned with matters of authenticity is clear throughout this volume. One of the pioneering initiatives on business and professional discourse is the Wellington Language in the Workplace Project, which Holmes & Vine write about extensively in their contribution to this volume. It is interesting to note that they revisit the Project essentially as a case of workplace research and applications *in real world contexts*. When it began in 1996, the main goal was to explore "authentic workplace interaction" (this volume, p. 26). Crucially, there is an assumption here not that research on workplace interaction was particularly new but that the workplace interaction that had been researched so far was intrinsically non-authentic. Holmes & Vine go on to specify what they mean by authentic workplace interaction: it is, they say, about "everyday interactions between co-workers and other people with whom they interact at work" (this volume, p. 26). Here, interestingly, authentic can be taken to equal 'everyday'.

As for the everyday nature of the interactions, it is important to note that the Project's methodology for data collection originally included volunteers recording a range of their interactions in their workplaces over a period of about a month. In discussing how authentic such data are, Holmes & Vine note that after less than 10 minutes participants typically forgot about the recording equipment "as they became engrossed in their *normal* workplace interactions" (this volume, p. 30—our italics), thus reducing the effect of the "observer's paradox" (Labov 1972, p. 209) where individuals tend to be self-conscious and thus impact on the data when being observed. Holmes & Vine conclude that they can be confident that the recordings provided a large amount of authentic interaction, even when this includes adopting the so-called "mystery shopper" technique for studying service encounters.

In looking back at the origins of the Project, Holmes & Vine are especially eager to differentiate the study of authentic workplace interaction from research on workplace interaction which uses interview or survey data. It is argued that "research based on authentic talk produces a much richer appreciation of workplace communication than using staged interactions or just interviewing people about their communication practices. What people *think* they do and what they *actually* do can be quite different" (this volume, p. 48).

A similar view of authenticity is held by Tanaka who, in his contribution to the present volume, argues that most research on global communication competence, intercultural competence, and communicative competence relies on self-report or what he calls 'second-hand data'. These are data collected by means of survey methods and interviews. In Tanaka's opinion they are a poor alternative to 'first-hand' data, which he qualifies as naturally occurring and which, in many cases, seem just too difficult to get hold of, both logistically and ethically.

Tanaka's chapter is focused on an alternative approach to recording spontaneous data as it raises the question of authenticity in business discourse data and the extent to which simulations can evidence real-time communicative events in critical-incident cases. He reports on a case where Japanese researchers needed what he terms 'authentic' critical incident scenarios to be able to develop a situational judgment test of global business discourse competence (GBDC) for Japanese business practitioners. Such critical incident scenarios, Tanaka continues, rely on naturally occurring data, but these are very difficult to get hold of as incidents are, by their very nature, unpredictable and data collection is further hampered by privacy and confidentiality concerns. That's why, following Van Maanen's idea of ethnographic 'realist tales' (1988), he devised a series of so-called 'simulated vignettes' using data from multiple sources including interviews, focus group meetings and surveys and drawing on feedback from subject matter specialists and pre-test test takers. Tanaka explains how, in doing so, he employed data collected from multiple sources and how "[the vignettes'] authenticity was continually revised through review and dialogue with stakeholders until their authenticity was verified" (this volume, p. 118). It's a series of iterative, cyclical processes of data collection and analysis involving focus group meetings with a so-called 'development committee' made up of senior HRD directors from four multinational business corporations who need to "ratify" or even "validate" the data, followed by an extensive online survey (n = 300). The main question in Tanaka's chapter is therefore "whether business discourse data can be simulated authentically" (this volume, p. 118), in particular whether critical incidents that were scripted on the basis of second-hand data and acted out by carefully auditioned professional performers with substantial business experience can be considered authentic.

While Tanaka is by no means the first to look at how to integrate simulations of real cases in pedagogical settings (see for example Drury-Grogan and Russ 2013), we believe that his self-reflection on how 'effective', 'close to reality', 'realistic', quasi-authentic' and 'ethical' they are in 'enhancing authenticity' and 'reproducing' authentic critical incidents is particularly innovative in the context of this volume's quest to find out what counts as good data in business and professional discourse research and training.

Not all work on business and professional discourse starts from the strict view of authenticity that was sketched above, though. In this volume, Holmes & Vine's and Tanaka's views of interview data as essentially non-authentic are not shared in either Efthymiadou's and Jacobs & Vandendaele's contributions.

Efthymiadou, to begin with, writes about what she calls 'linguistic authenticity', tying in with a long-standing concern in sociolinguistic research with 'real language', meaning language that is produced by authentic speakers in authentic communicative situations (Bucholtz 2003). One key notion that has dominated the analysis of discourse for decades now (and that both Holmes & Vine's and Tanaka's chapters start from) is that of 'naturally occurring speech', with interactions spontaneously unfolding as part of the everyday life of people and not as a result of pre-arranged conditions. Efthymiadou goes on to explain that in this respect sociolinguists have positioned themselves in different ways in relation to authenticity and the legitimacy of interview and focus-group data. Some, for example those in Conversation Analysis, insist on what they call 'actual' data and argue that what comes out of interviews or focus groups is 'manufactured' or, worse, 'compromised'. Others have argued that all discourse data is produced, or 'got up' for something, and so, in their view, interview and focus-group data are not more compromised than any other, so-called 'natural' talk. In the end, they argue, no truly authentic data is possible. Or, in a more positive light, the social constructionist lens described above makes us look at interviews as meaning-making and knowledge-building processes, just like any other, seemingly more natural interactions. In the study that she reports on in her chapter in this volume Efthymiadou strongly aligns with the latter group viewing interviews as situated action (Cicourel 1964) or social practice (Talmy 2011) that is valuable in its own right. She argues that interview data can be a legitimate and valuable source of information in ethnographic projects, despite the influence of the researcher's presence on the interaction at hand.

More or less the same can be said of Jacobs & Vandendaele's contribution to this volume. Following up on earlier case-based explorations of the complex interactions between learning, research, and practice in the field of business and professional communication (Bruyer et al. 2016; Vandendaele et al. 2016), they zoom in on interviewing and raise a number of questions on the use of collective data-gathering techniques as part of a wider, multi-site study on the multilingual workplace. Their dataset consists of the transcripts of the audio-recordings of 65 semi-structured interviews conducted by graduate students of business communication in the organizations where they were about to start their traineeships (including corporate and non-profit settings and ranging from small start-ups to long-established multi-department companies). In addition to demonstrating how multilingualism is embraced as a strategic asset within the broader framework of glocalization and multinational marketing, Jacobs & Vandendaele also speak to this volume's central question "What counts as good data?" and shed interesting new light on the affordances of collective data-gathering by identifying three distinct interviewer personae as well as a number of complex patterns of role-switching and identity construction.

From this perspective, Jacobs & Vandendaele's study can be seen as an experiment in collective data-gathering with the student-interviewers negotiating hybrid researcher-practitioner-learner identities. Drawing on an analysis of (varying degrees of) agency, lexical patterns and register, they observe a lot of diversity in the form of inter-interviewer variation. They argue that the three interviewer personae they identified (researcher—student—practitioner) do not constitute fixed and clearly delineated categories, but that, instead, that there is a continuum of identity construction with some students in the same category identifying to a greater or lesser extent with a particular persona than others. They add that this corresponds with what came out of their previous work on how to bridge the classroom and real-world practice in the area of business and professional communication (Vandendaele et al. 2016), where they point to the challenges involved in bringing together the worlds of learning, scholarship and practice and single out the same two parameters, viz. freedom and mutuality, that seem to distinguish them, with the researcher persona showing more freedom (e.g. vis-à-vis the script to be followed) than the student persona and the practitioner persona showing more mutuality (e.g. partnering up with the interviewee).

All of the above ties in with the key notion of authenticity that we started our discussion with: since the data gathering was subcontracted to the students, it could be argued that the data discussed in this study are—from the analysts' point of view at least—second-hand, hence not 100 percent authentic as there is a gap between the researchers and the practitioners that prevents us from reaching a deep understanding of what is going on in the interviews. Jacobs & Vandendaele's chapter is open-ended in this respect: they call for "a more comprehensive discussion on how researchers can collaborate and share results, and on how researcher positioning is affected" (this volume, p. 163). Such a discussion, they say, is especially pertinent when it comes to the complex interactions between scholars, learners and practitioners, where identities are fluid and boundaries get blurred.

A similar, broader view of what counts as good data can be seen in Andrews' contribution to this volume. The underlying hypothesis of her larger project is that business and professional discourse "occurs, by definition, in the context of work and the workplace" and hence that the physical environment of an office "shapes, reflects, and sometimes subverts the kind of communication required to get work done there" (this volume, p. 171). That's why she visited a range of workplaces, especially coworking spaces. Crucially, her dataset is based on both formal and informal interviews she conducted with practitioners as well as on extensive readings, not only in the academic but also in the commercial literature of workplace design. For the research reported here she actually looks at a number of online pitches which she had originally wanted to discard presumably because they could not be considered sufficiently authentic. In other words, Andrews starts out from a contrast between the reality of what is happening in the physical space and the not-so-real language and images on the websites. Elsewhere in her chapter she labels the latter "rhetorical"; they can be seen as *representations*, often highly "celebratory" (Gandini 2015), of the coworking spaces that she is interested in, but—Andrews concludes—this doesn't mean that they are not "worth attention" (this volume, p. 170): even if the concept of co-working itself may simply reflect an "illusory enthusiasm" used for "branding, marketing and business purposes" (Gandini, pp. 202–203), it's the creation of that illusion that matters for Andrews.

From Andrews's online pitches for co-working spaces, it is—in some way, at least—a small step to Domenec & Millot's chapter, where the analytical lens shifts to professional magazines for the domains of ethics management and of information and records management. The authors argue that they are relevant "as an entry point into specialization" for two reasons, viz. because their language is specialized, they provide us with a unique starting point to "grasp the culture and domain-specific expectations of the professional milieu under study" and because—on a more basic but by no means less important level—they are issued by and for professionals (this volume, p. 58), and this is what makes them authentic. Just like Andrews, Domenec & Millot are concerned with the fact that professional magazines are meant to convey a promotional, predominantly positive picture of the specialized communities in question and that this can be seen to make them less real, less natural or less authentic. For example, they point to the fact that many of the articles in them are shared on the professional network LinkedIn by the authors in order to present themselves as experts. Domenec & Millot conclude that this implies that the magazines "do not entirely represent business realities in these domains" (this volume, p. 67).

Triangulation

Many studies in business and professional discourse research adopt a triangulated approach, but it is often not explicitly explained how and/or why this approach has been adopted. In line with Angouri (2010), Varpio et al. (2017), and Hashemi and Babaii (2013), we argue that it is important to address this when presenting one's research, and the chapters in this volume serve as examples of how this can be done.

The fact that the term triangulation is not consistently used among researchers and can be used to mean different things (Angouri 2010) makes it all the more relevant to explicitly mention one's own understanding and application of the term. As Angouri (2010, p. 34) states based on the work of Denzin (1970, p. 472), triangulation most commonly refers to data triangulation (the application of more than one sampling method for data collection) and methodological triangulation (the use of more than one methodology), but two additional types of triangulation can be distinguished, viz. investigator triangulation (the involvement of more than one researcher) and theoretical triangulation (the use of more than one theoretical perspective). While this distinction between different types of triangulation is still easy to grasp, matters become more complicated when considering the relationship between the terms triangulation and mixed methods research. On the one hand, data and methodological triangulation are often used as synonyms of the term 'mixed methods'. On the other hand, however, some scholars use triangulation in a more narrow sense—based on the original use of the term in the context of navigation (Varpio et al. 2017; Hashemi and Babaii 2013)—, as one possible purpose of a mixed methods approach, based on Greene et al.'s (1989) categorization of five mixed methods purposes (as cited in Angouri 2010, p. 35): "*initiation*—aiming at discovering meaningful contradictions and 'the paradox'; *complementarity*—aiming at shedding light on different aspects of the same phenomenon; *development*—aiming at using findings elicited by the use of one method for the design of the second or subsequent one; *expansion*—aiming at broadening the scope and objective of the research"; and *triangulation*—aiming at convergence of findings and corroboration and validation of research results. According to this distinction of five purposes for mixed methods research, triangulation is a purpose which aligns with positivist and post-positivist perspectives on research rigour (Varpio et al. 2017), as it is based on the assumption that, ideally, research findings obtained through different methods converge to one single objective 'reality' or 'truth', and if this is not the case, those findings cannot be validated. This also means that in its narrow sense, triangulation is not compatible with a mixed methods purpose such as initiation, which, in opening itself up to divergent perspectives on a phenomenon, aligns with a non-positivist, social constructionist view on rigour as an ontological and epistemological stance, with rigour being achieved "through comprehensiveness rather than convergence" (Varpio et al. 2017, p. 5). The contributions in this volume use the term triangulation in its broader sense, as a synonym of mixed methods research encompassing all its possible purposes.

In the case of mixed methods research (or data and/or method triangulation in the broader sense), it often—but not always—concerns a combination of qualitative and quantitative (data collection) methods (Bazeley 2008). In this volume, the contributions by Tanaka and by Domenec & Millot both report on a mixed methods design incorporating both quantitative and qualitative approaches. The fact that they combine these approaches in their overall research design is not surprising, given their affiliation with research fields in which such designs have grown popular: the fields of intercultural communication (Tanaka) and English for Specific Purposes (Domenec & Millot). Tanaka, in reflecting on the wide body of intercultural communication research, sees substantial merit in integrating both approaches as a means to overcome the limitations of either. The risk of bias in self-report data obtained through surveys, for instance, can be offset by ethnographic observations of naturally occurring interactions. In the actual design of his study, however, although it combines qualitative (focus group meetings, interviews) and quantitative (surveys) data collection methods, naturally occurring data could not be obtained for the reasons explained above. This shows how it is also the setting—in this context the workplace—that can influence the methods that a researcher is able to employ (Angouri 2010). Domenec & Millot, for their part, mainly discuss the results of a corpus-based quantitative study, but they frame this study as part of a larger project on professional discourses, and they argue that a complete characterization of a professional domain should include other datasets, like research articles (to take into account the theory of the domain) as well as onsite surveys, interviews and other ethnographic studies (to explore practices in the field). The latter can be read as an explicit call to expand data collection and analysis to the context of production and circulation of professional knowledge.

One can still speak of mixed methods when it concerns a combination of only qualitative techniques, as is the case in several contributions in this volume (Holmes & Vine; Efthymiadou; Andrews). It is especially typical of studies adopting an interactional sociolinguistic perspective (Holmes & Vine; Efthymiadou) to collect different types of qualitative data, with a focus on naturally occurring interactions on the one hand and interviews on the other. Holmes & Vine stress the usefulness of interviews in helping the researchers gain a better understanding of the naturally occurring data and the context in which it was collected. Interviews, in their view, can assist with the interpretation and analysis of the recorded data, providing contextualization to a methodology that is fundamentally geared towards capturing 'authenticity' (see above). Recordings (and transcripts, for that matter) can be taken back to participants for discussion and 'confirmation' purposes. As Holmes & Vine indicate, such feedback sessions "proved very worthwhile both for us as analysts and for the participants who consistently commented on how interesting and insightful the discussion proved for them as well" (this volume, p. 31). Efthymiadou too acknowledges that interviews can be used as a complementary source of data alongside other methods (e.g. conducting retrospective or follow-up interviews to shed light on participants' understandings of recorded events), but what distinguishes her take on interviews from that of Holmes & Vine is that she insists that in her project the 20 semi-structured interviews do not have to be seen as an add-on to the audio and video recordings of naturally occurring interactions that are also in her dataset. Crucially, she argues, one is not 'more appropriate' than the other; they simply shed light on different dimensions of her central research focus, viz. doing trust.

Aside from data and method triangulation, theoretical triangulation also plays a role in some of this volume's chapters (Andrews; Holmes & Vine). Andrews incorporates theoretical and methodological insights from material culture studies (which examines the relationship between people and the things around them), design thinking (linking space, innovation, aesthetics and collaboration) and the rhetoric of business and professional communication (the ancient art of persuasion, here "refreshed to provide strategies for representing these new work environments", this volume, p. 172), while Holmes & Vine do the same for interactional sociolinguistics and leadership studies. While theoretical triangulation can be quite challenging, especially when it boils down to an interdisciplinary approach, it can also, according to Holmes & Vine (this volume, p. 32) prove "very rewarding in terms of new insights and applications."

Background

When the affordances of qualitative and quantitative approaches are discussed in the context of mixed methods research, qualitative approaches are generally associated with the ability to enhance, deepen and enrich our understanding of specific phenomena. Essential in this regard, as it can be seen as a prerequisite in reaching such a level of understanding, is undoubtedly the notion of background. This notion has been widely discussed in the literature on business and professional discourse. The current volume is no exception.

Domenec & Millot, to begin with, label their approach as context-oriented, i.e. with a focus on language in context. They chose professional magazines as an entry point into specialization because these texts display specialized language in action and can thus be used to grasp the specific specialized context under study, and because they are part of writing practices in these specialized settings. By analyzing a wide-ranging set of features in their specialized corpus, features that include domain-specific collocational patterns, mediation strategies and metaphorical language and that allow for communicating specialized knowledge to the members of a specific professional community, they are able to reveal different degrees of specialization in their data, ranging from general (so-called 'low specializedness') to specific ('high specializedness' linked to a specific business context).

Tanaka also zooms in on the notion of background when he indicates that most InterCultural Interaction Competency (ICIC) tests currently available are criticized for their cultural bias. In particular, they tend to overgeneralize competence as locally specific contextual and environmental factors are ignored. Tanaka refers to the broader sociolinguistic concern with the "contextual situatedness of linguistic competence" (Blommaert et al. 2005, p. 197).

In their conclusion, Jacobs & Vandendaele argue that coming to grips with what they call the "essential contextedness" of all business and professional discourse is a key requirement, no matter if the study is focused on multilingualism in Belgian organizations or on something completely different. "Any data, including audio and video recordings, interview transcripts or the results of survey research, are deeply and unavoidably embedded in the organizational context where they originate, and they are bound to entail profound power asymmetries that impact on what people say or write. It follows that standardized data (where data are perfectly comparable across settings) is not just a myth in business and professional discourse studies; it's not even desirable. Instead, the intrinsic diversity of the discursive repertoire constitutes a rich basis for analysis in its own right" (this volume, p. 162).

Every context also comes with its own specific power constellations, which need to be taken into account when analyzing and interpreting the data. In exploring the history of the Wellington project Holmes & Vine indicate that they first approached workplaces which were similar to their own (i.e., white-collar, professional, government offices) since they assumed the researchers were more familiar with features of the workplace cultures in such contexts. Later blue-collar workplaces were also included in the research with data from factories; at the same time, on the internal v. external communication axis, recordings of interaction between colleagues were supplemented with interaction with outsiders, including nurse-patient dialogues. Jacobs & Vandendaele indicate that their data are exclusively related to white-collar settings: as the interviews that their students conducted are with managers or senior office staff only, they realize they may well have missed out on some of the more critical views about multilingualism that exist elsewhere in the workplace, especially in blue-collar environments (e.g. Lønsmann 2014).

As the different stances taken up by researchers depending on their research environments (e.g., white-collar or blue-collar) show, power asymmetries not only need to be studied as part of the data itself, but they are also relevant when reflecting on the relationship between researchers and their objects of study, and on the data collection process itself. It is important for researchers to respect their research participants, for instance by claiming agency for the professionals whose words are recorded and subsequently analysed or by critically reflecting on one's own role as a researcher in interactions with participants. Holmes & Vine write about framing the research as taking place *with* rather than *on* participants in this respect, and interviews in particular play a major role in such a process of empowerment and self-reflection. In her chapter Efthymiadou zooms in on one of the first interviews with her main informant and she dissects how her presence undeniably affected the way the interview unfolded and how, instead of compromising the data, it led to valuable insights about the informant's positioning and self-representation that so-called naturally occurring data wouldn't have allowed. Overall, Efthymiadou's chapter is a powerful illustration of how a detailed and in-depth discussion on researcher positioning is closely related to questions about the quality of the data collected and about analytical rigour.

As researchers form part of the research process, any discussion on data authenticity should also involve reflection on the role of the researcher in the research process, including the ways in which the researcher is perceived by participants.

Reflecting on the way in which interviewers position themselves in interactions with practitioners is also key to Jacobs & Vandendaele's contribution. They used a collective data-gathering technique by means of student-led interviews, and argue that researchers need to be aware of 'inter-interviewer variation', which they address as a research question in its own right. They go on to suggest that genuine awareness of this diversity implies recognizing that the interviews are deeply embedded in the program's traineeship efforts and acknowledging the power dimension involved in this. This includes mapping how confident students are in the process of negotiating access, gaining trust and constructing a professional identity for themselves (one that may or may not be in conflict with their role as students/researchers).

To end this section on understanding background, let's address an indirectly related but constantly recurring question: how much data is needed? The question of 'how much data we need' is mostly discussed through the concept of data saturation, which generally refers to the idea that data is saturated, i.e. no new data are needed, when no new themes emerge from the data or when the data yield no new insights which would alter the findings of a particular study. It can be argued, however, that such an idea of data saturation mainly applies to studies in which data is collected and analyzed iteratively and concurrently, following procedures as stipulated in Grounded Theory, and that it is much less applicable to research adopting a different approach. Moreover, there is also "a philosophical question about whether theories, data or themes can ever be truly saturated" (Varpio et al. 2017, p. 45). Against this background, a more interesting concept than data saturation might be the notion of information power (Malterud et al. 2016, p. 1): "Information power indicates that the more information the sample holds, relevant for the actual study, the lower amount of participants is needed", with the size of a sample with sufficient information power depending on "(a) the aim of the study, (b) sample specificity, (c) use of established theory, (d) quality of dialogue, and (e) analysis strategy." In general, ethnographic studies are believed to possess high information power because of the use of various methods and rich data. Andrews's sample as described in her contribution in this volume, however, can also, in view of her analytical strategy and the particular aim of her study, focusing on persuasive discourse in the context of texts advertising co-working spaces, be considered as high in information power.

It needs to be pointed out here that most chapters in this volume show a strong preference for oral interactional data. In this context Efthymiadou refers to a long-standing and deeply rooted preoccupation in sociolinguistics with transactional interactions, and small talk instances, including meeting processes of all kinds as they are taken to quintessentially reflect leadership styles, institutionalized power and authority relationships and rapport management (see for example Spencer-Oatey 2008). Some of the contributors do show an awareness of the potential of including multimodal data, however. Andrews, for example, argues that her larger project is specifically aimed at disrupting ongoing communications research by focusing less on what is said and done in a workplace and more on the agency of place itself in that activity. As for the study reported on in this volume, this results in what she sees as a 'major constraint' as she sets out to report her analysis of on-line, full-color co-working space pitches incorporating videos and music in a traditional text-based print medium. Similarly, connecting with the volume's overall focus, Domenec & Millot argue that one way in which they shed new light on what counts as good data in business and professional discourse and training is in pointing to an "enriched" dataset with technologies enabling researchers to add visualizing tools, images or videos, paving the way to ever thicker descriptions of professional discourse.

Relevance

A final key notion that is high on the agenda of all contributions to this volume is that of relevance. In exploring the history of the Wellington Language in the Workplace Project Holmes & Vine stress that "[a]t every point, a priority has been to make the findings of [their] research relevant to workplaces" (this volume, p. 45). This includes considering how authentic data can be used as input to a range of types of training resources. Throughout their chapter Holmes & Vine insist that the authenticity of their dataset is a prerequisite for applying the results of their work in the real world. That's why early on the Project turned to studying workplace miscommunication as well as the communication challenges encountered by new migrant workers, which were frequently the focus of New Zealand employers' concerns. Holmes & Vine are very explicit about giving back to the workplaces where they conduct their study, as they adopt an action research approach, encouraging employees to examine, evaluate and learn from their own communications.

The link between authenticity and relevance is perhaps even clearer when Holmes & Vine refer to learning, in particular the acquisition of pragmatic skills, where providing formulaic responses for a necessarily limited range of contexts is offset against helping students to analyse real-life examples, to identify critical social relationships and contextual factors, and—ultimately—to cope with the world out there. It is interesting to note in this context that, in terms of output, Holmes & Vine refer to the need to reach beyond academic journals and scholarly books with their technical analysis and specialised linguistic jargon, and to provide more widely accessible materials.

Jacobs & Vandendaele are equally preoccupied with relevance when they argue that "[w]hat distinguishes research on business and professional discourse perhaps most from other scholarly endeavours in the realm of language and communication is the very thin line between practice and learning" (this volume, p. 143). At the same time, they indicate that students typically struggle to forge a sustainable partnership with practitioners, e.g. in trying to translate their academic research in useful and practice-driven recommendations (see e.g. Vandendaele et al. 2016).

Domenec & Millot too insist that their scholarly efforts are useful to professionals as the professional magazines they study display "practical relevance" and focus on "topics and phenomena with which practitioners in the field are actually confronted" (Wolf and Rosenberg 2012, p. 181). Hence, analyzing them is bound to help gain insight into specific "professional logics" (Demont 2013, p. 9). Domenec & Millot also think of training in business and professional discourse when they argue that the articles in their professional magazines can be studied in class or that they might even be used as a basis for case studies, role plays or specialized translation exercises.

A couple of comments are in order here. First of all, it can be argued that it is at this point that relevance may well conflict with authenticity, especially when it comes to training purposes. Holmes & Vine, for example, explain in quite some detail how they used recordings of role-plays and interviews as part of their training materials in the domain of ethnicity and professional migrants' acquisition of and adaptation to New Zealand interactional pragmatics. Likewise, Tanaka's efforts to develop a situational judgment test of global business discourse competence (GBDC) for Japanese business practitioners leads him towards developing less than fully authentic critical incident scenarios.

Secondly, the need for relevance that is a concern throughout the chapters in this volume seems to suggest that the analytical focus is not on the workplace in its own right, as a type of institutionalized discourse intrinsically worth studying. Instead, there appears to be consensus that looking at workplace interaction is a good thing to do for the very simple reason that it can help solve problems. This is not to say that relevance is restricted to how people use language at work to accomplish transactional goals. Holmes & Vine, for example, also look at the various ways in which to maintain and develop good workplace relationships. Similarly, Domenec & Millot argue that one reason why the professional magazines they study are relevant is that "just like academic journals which contribute to the making of disciplines, [they] play a major role in the construction and evolution of professions. As a genre set, they aim not only to transmit specialized knowledge to a given professional community, but they also help build the identity of the professional community, through the circulation and evolution of specialized language" (this volume, pp. 57–58). It is interesting in this respect that Holmes & Vine situate their scholarly efforts within the broader framework of interactional sociolinguistics, which—in their view—is especially concerned with investigating linguistic and cultural diversity, but where ultimately "the *relevance* of the research being undertaken is an important basic consideration" (this volume, p. 35).

Note, finally, that relevance and the notion of giving back to the professionals under scrutiny are an important argument in negotiating access. Holmes & Vine indicate how spelling out the potential benefits of their research to the workplace was a major factor in convincing professionals to volunteer to carry recording equipment. It is in this context that we can look at the distinct preference for success that characterizes a lot of research about workplace discourse. Holmes & Vine point out that theirs was a deliberate decision to focus on successful and effective communication as it encourages professionals to become involved and helps develop and maintain a relationship of trust. Again, prioritizing what goes well need not imply an exclusively transactional perspective: for Holmes & Vine and the Wellington Project, for example, focusing on success includes "attending to the relational or interpersonal dimension of interaction which ensures smooth collegial relationships" (this volume, p. 26). Their approach can be seen as an appreciative enquiry as they zoom in on the communicative and interactional practices of a professional called Greg, a "very consultative leader" who listens carefully, seeks out the opinions of others and does an excellent job hedging his own interventions. Just like Efthymiadou demonstrates how her informants negotiate trust, much of Holmes & Vine's analysis is about showing how, as a leader, Greg is particularly skilled at managing the relational dimensions of interaction.

It should be noted that, just like the ambition to be relevant, the focus on successful communication may be seen to run counter to the idea of authenticity, as unsuccessful communication tends to be put by the wayside or, worse, ignored. At the same time, the question can be raised if some of this does not come at the expense of a critical inquiry into what constitutes professional (or communicative) success, if—for example—there is perhaps no a priori assumption what smooth collegial relationships are.

It is difficult to summarize what the discussion on authenticity, triangulation, background and relevance in this introductory chapter ultimately entails for the question what counts as good data. Perhaps one possible answer points away from the data as such, in the direction of the researcher: it could be argued that what the various studies in this volume demonstrate is that a fair degree of what can be called 'ethnographic sensitivity' is essential to all business and professional discourse research and training. Based on their investigation of the interfaces between learning, research and practice via the analysis of a student research project on Corporate Social Responsibility (CSR) in the pharmaceutical industry, Bruyer et al. (2016) already called for an ethnographer's perspective, with—in their case—an increased student awareness of their unique insider position as 'junior consultants' for the organizations. Following up in the present volume, Jacobs & Vandendaele reflect on the double role of the internship encapsulated in the fact that it can be approached as a fieldwork experience, allowing for a combination of (reflexive) ethnography and (hands-on, action-oriented) practice. All of the other chapters in this volume point to the same implication for how students, scholars and practitioners can work together in researching the many complexities of language in the workplace, one that can be taken to serve as a guideline in order to strengthen interaction between them: by displaying an ethnographic sensitivity that reconciles relevance with a broad take on authenticity, that values a wide range of data, that empowers all involved in the research process and that pursues a deep understanding of the rich context of the workplace.

References

Alessi, G. M., & Jacobs, G. (Eds.). (2016). *The ins and outs of business and professional discourse research: Reflections on interacting with the workplace*. London: Palgrave Macmillan.

Angouri, J. (2010). Quantitative, qualitative or both? Combining methods in linguistic research. In L. Litosseliti (Ed.), *Research methods in linguistics* (Vol. 1, pp. 29–45). New York: Continuum.

Bazeley, P. (2008). Mixed methods in management research. In R. Holt & R. Thorpe (Eds.), *Dictionary of qualitative management research* (pp. 133–136). London: Sage.

Blommaert, J., Collins, J., & Slembrouck, S. (2005). Spaces of multilingualism. *Language & Communication.*, *25*, 197–216.

Bruyer, T., Jacobs, G., & Vandendaele, A. (2016). Good pharma? How business communication research can help bridge the gap between students and practitioners. *Business and Professional Communication Quarterly*, *79*, 141–153.

Bucholtz, M. (2003). *Sociolinguistic nostalgia and identity*. Oxford: Blackwell.

Cicourel, A. V. (1964). *Method and measurement in sociology*. New York: Free Press.

Demont, G. (2013). L'éthique professionnelle peut-elle se penser au singulier ? Le cas des formations dans le secteur de l'aide à la personne dépendante. *Recherche et pratiques pédagogiques en langues de spécialité*. https://doi.org/10.4000/apliut.3773.

Denzin, N. K. (Ed.). (1970). *The research act in sociology: A theoretical introduction to sociological method*. New York: McGraw-Hill.

Drury-Grogan, M. L., & Russ, T. L. (2013). A contemporary simulation infused in the business communication curriculum: A case study. *Business Communication Quarterly, 76*, 304–321.

Gandini, A. (2015). The rise of coworking spaces: A literature review. *Ephemera: Theory and politics in organization, 15*, 193–205.

Greene, J. C., Caracelli, V. J., & Graham, W. F. (1989). Toward a conceptual framework for mixed-method evaluation designs. *Educational Evaluation and Policy Analysis, 11*, 255–274.

Hashemi, M. R., & Babaii, E. (2013). Mixed methods research: Toward new research designs in applied linguistics. *Modern Language Journal, 97*, 828–852.

Hodgkinson, G. P., & Rousseau, D. M. (2009). Bridging the rigour–relevance gap in management research: It's already happening! *Journal of Management Studies, 46*, 534–546.

Kieser, A., & Leiner, L. (2009). Why the rigour–relevance gap in management research is unbridgeable. *Journal of Management Studies, 4*, 516–533.

Labov, W. (1972). *Sociolinguistic patterns*. Philadelphia: University of Pennsylvania.

Lønsmann, D. (2014). Linguistic diversity in the international workplace: Language ideologies and processes of exclusion. *Multilingua—Journal of Cross-Cultural and Interlanguage Communication, 33*, 89–116.

Malterud, K., Siersma, V. D., & Guassora, A. D. (2016). Sample size in qualitative interview studies: Guided by information power. *Qualitative Health Research, 26*, 1753–1760.

Spencer-Oatey, H. (2008). *Culturally speaking: Culture, communication and politeness theory*. London: Continuum.

Talmy, S. (2011). The interview as collaborative achievement: Interaction, identity, and ideology in a speech event. *Applied Linguistics, 32*, 25–42.

Van Leeuwen, T. (2001). What is authenticity? *Discourse Studies, 3*, 392–397.

Van Maanen, J. (1988). *Tales of the field: On writing ethnography*. Chicago: University of Chicago Press.

Vandendaele, A., Bruyer, T., & Jacobs, G. (2016). We never even wondered whether we trusted them or not: From freedom to mutuality in a student research project. In G. M. Alessi & G. Jacobs (Eds.), *The ins and outs of business and professional discourse research : Reflections on interacting with the workplace* (pp. 102–116). London: Palgrave Macmillan.

Varpio, L., Ajjawi, R., Monrouxe, L. V., O'Brien, B. C., & Rees, C. E. (2017). Shedding the cobra effect: Problematising thematic emergence, triangulation, saturation and member checking. *Medical Education, 51*, 40–50.

Wolf, J., & Rosenberg, T. (2012). How individual scholars can reduce the rigor-relevance gap in management research. *Business Research, 5*, 178–196.

2

Workplace Research and Applications in Real World Contexts: The Case of the Wellington Language in the Workplace Project

Janet Holmes and Bernadette Vine

Introduction

When the Language in the Workplace (LWP) Project began in 1996, our main goal was to describe the language of a domain that had been largely neglected in studies of New Zealand English. Having collected a one-million-word corpus of formal and informal spoken New Zealand English (Holmes et al. 1998), and undertaken the first systematic social dialect survey of New Zealand English (Holmes et al. 1991), we became very aware that workplace talk was a neglected area of study. This was not just a local problem; linguistic research on workplace discourse internationally was sparse and mainly confined to studies of medical and legal discourse (see e.g. Drew and Heritage 1992). We were also conscious that researching authentic workplace communication had a great deal of

J. Holmes (✉) • B. Vine
School of Linguistics and Applied Language Studies, Victoria University of Wellington, Wellington, New Zealand
e-mail: Janet.Holmes@vuw.ac.nz; Bernadette.Vine@vuw.ac.nz

G. Jacobs, S. Decock (eds.), *Good Data in Business and Professional Discourse Research and Teaching*, Communicating in Professions and Organizations,
https://doi.org/10.1007/978-3-030-61757-8_2

potential for applying the results of our work in the real world, since workplace miscommunication as well as the communication challenges encountered by new migrant workers were frequently the focus of New Zealand employers' concerns. With these two goals in mind we began to research New Zealand workplace discourse.[1]

We first approached workplaces which were similar to our own (i.e., white-collar, professional, government offices) since we felt that we were likely to be more familiar with features of the workplace cultures in such contexts. We also made a deliberate decision to focus on successful communication, that is, to study how people manage to communicate effectively at work. Hence our first publications examined how people achieve their transactional goals in such workplaces, whilst also attending to the relational or interpersonal dimension of interaction which ensures smooth collegial relationships (Holmes et al. 1999; Holmes 2000a, b, c; Holmes and Marra 2002).

It soon became apparent that our work had a range of possible applications, not only for speakers of English as a first language who faced communication problems in their workplaces, but also for English as a second language learners and especially recent immigrants to New Zealand (Holmes 2005, 2019). As our work developed, so did the potential for applying it to a wider range of real-world contexts. This chapter documents some of the main steps on the research journey we have undertaken since 1996. We describe the main features of the methodology we have developed to collect good quality authentic workplace discourse from a wide range of contexts and outline our theoretical framework. This is followed by some examples of how we analyse our data. Finally, some applications of our work in the real world are briefly discussed.

It will be clear as this story unfolds that three of the four central themes identified in this volume were key concerns for the LWP project: authenticity, triangulation and background. We aimed to collect authentic workplace interaction, which for us meant everyday interactions between co-workers and other people with whom they interact at work. Research on workplace interaction which uses interview or survey data can of course provide useful insights, but if we want to know *how* people interact examining authentic interaction is invaluable. We also felt that in order to gain a better understanding of the data and each context in which it was collected, we needed to gather other types of data, as well as consulting with workplace participants and experts in other areas. A number of distinctive aspects of the project have helped us in achieving these goals: the aim to research *with* rather than *on* participants, the adaptations to our methodology when working with participants in different workplaces, and the growth of an interdisciplinary team whose members have worked fruitfully together.

A fifth aspect that the editors of this volume highlight in their introduction is the rigour-relevance debate in management studies (see e.g. Hodgkinson and Rousseau 2009; Kieser and Leiner 2009; Wolf and Rosenberg 2012). This relates to criticisms of management research as not "sufficiently considering the practical relevance of their research, and of merely pursuing scientific rigor instead" (Wolf and Rosenberg 2012, p. 178). Within the field of sociolinguistics, there has for many decades been a strong sub-field focussed on applications of research to language-related real life problems.

Gaining Access to Workplaces

A first issue we consider in terms of our methodology is how we gain access to workplaces. It is not easy to get into workplaces to record, but collecting data in NZ is probably easier than many other countries because of the small population and the emphasis on informality. Access to each workplace was arranged in advance with personal contacts being crucial to gaining entry. The idea of six degrees of separation between any two people on the planet (Karinthy 1929) is more like two or three degrees in New Zealand. Later on our established reputation often helped in gaining access to additional workplaces.

The key to access therefore was usually finding a workplace where someone we knew worked who could vouch for our integrity and the value we could offer. The project started with an organisation where Janet Holmes had a good friend in a senior role who persuaded the CEO to allow Janet to come and talk first to her and then to the Senior Management Team about what we wanted to do and why.

The fact that as a respected university professor Janet Holmes had high status was also relevant. We found that it was important to use a high status person for the initial contact as this meant that people took the proposal seriously. Janet's status as a researcher within New Zealand, and the fact that she was known in the wider community through media and other public engagement, certainly smoothed access on many occasions.

Often a seminar on communication issues was presented as a first step when proposing to work with a new organisation so that potential collaborators could become familiar with the type of work that we do. With the first organisation we worked with Janet offered and delivered a seminar to the whole organization on a topic of interest to them—language and gender (as it was an organization committed to improving social conditions for women). Following the presentations, Janet talked about what we were hoping to do and what benefits we hoped to offer a workplace or team in the form of insights about their communication patterns. The first organisation we worked with responded enthusiastically after the initial seminar and four volunteers offered to carry recording equipment immediately.

Every organisation we approached was provided with written material outlining our aims and highlighting the results of previously completed research. In writing this material, we avoided jargon, making our research accessible for a non-specialist audience, and foregrounding issues which we hoped would be of interest to workplace participants.

Once one organization had agreed to cooperate, we found that others were more likely to do so. Some are happy to have their cooperation mentioned, while others prefer to remain anonymous. We guarantee anonymity if that is what they want and we promise that no individuals will be identified. This is a vital step in establishing a trusting relationship between our project team and workplace teams we work with.

We have consistently adopted an appreciative enquiry approach in our research (Cooperrider et al. 2003), exploring effective workplace communication strategies and highlighting what people do well. This too encourages workplaces to become involved and helps develop and maintain a relationship of trust.

Another vital aspect of our methodology has been our commitment to working *with* rather than researching *on* participants and the goals and interests of the workplaces were consequently always incorporated into our planning (see Vine 2016, p. 326). A few central questions that workplaces always wanted us to address from a practical perspective were:

- what was in it for them?, i.e., benefits
- what costs were involved? (e.g. people's time)
- could we guarantee that the data would be treated as confidential?

This approach has been very productive for the LWP though inevitably there have also been rebuffs along the way, often for confidentiality reasons. Others considered they were too busy at the time we approached them, and/or that being involved in research would be too disruptive. But overall, we were very gratified by the number of workplaces who welcomed our interest and subsequently expressed appreciation for the feedback we provided to them.

Collecting Data

Although the focus of the data collection has changed over the years depending on our current theoretical interests, the basic approach has remained the same: volunteers record a range of their everyday interactions in their workplaces over a period of about a month. Data collection typically commences after a period of observation, where a research assistant, in consultation with workers, identifies the most fruitful places to collect data (e.g. the meeting room, offices, morning tea room), and assesses the best method of data collection for the specific workplace (e.g. fixed cameras, volunteers with recording devices on their desks or person). The research assistants are typically not present during the recording stage; the participants themselves take control of the recorders to collect their interactions.

This approach to recording has a number of advantages, including reducing the effect of the "observer's paradox" (Labov 1972, p. 209) i.e. the research problem posed by the tendency for individuals to be very self-conscious when being observed. It also gives control and agency to the workers whose words are recorded, a crucial component of our research methodology. Our extensive experience established that after a very short time (e.g. 10 minutes at most) participants forgot about the recording equipment as they became engrossed in their normal workplace interactions. Though they occasionally remembered (e.g. when someone swore), overall we were confident that the recordings provided a large amount of authentic interaction. We were told on numerous occasions by workplace participants how recording just became part of their work routine as they focussed on achieving workplace goals, e.g. decision-making or problem-solving.

Wherever possible, we triangulate our data sources to assist in interpretation and analysis. The ethnographic notes made by our research assistants during the observation phase before recording started always provide invaluable background information about the norms and practices in different workplaces. Data collection is followed by individual interviews and/or discussions with groups to elicit their views about the communication patterns identified and the analysis we have undertaken. Participants provide insights into workplace norms and typically they have supported the conclusions and findings of our research, highlighting the importance and value of this step in the research process. Enabling participants to take active roles in the research through consultation at many stages, as well as giving them control of recording, means that we have also developed some very productive research partnerships. In one case, for example, we were able to offer methodological advice and training support for a project being developed by one of our research partners. In other cases, we have cooperated in joint analysis and publication (Holmes and Fillary 2000; Kell et al. 2007; Vine et al. 2009).

Our methodology was innovative when first developed. To summarise, we negotiated with workplaces to permit recordings of everyday workplace talk. We convinced volunteers to work with us and record their mundane workplace interactions. Triangulation in the form of an initial period of ethnographic observation and post-recording interviews assisted with interpretation and analysis of the recorded data. Whenever possible we took recordings and transcripts back to participants for discussion, especially where we were unsure of our analysis or wished for confirmation of our interpretation of some aspect of interaction. Such sessions proved very worthwhile both for us as analysts and for the participants who consistently commented on how interesting and insightful the discussion proved for them as well. In addition we workshopped material with workplace teams who were agreeable to this offer, and again the resulting insights undoubtedly benefitted both us as researchers and the participants.

Data Collected and Adaptations to Methodology

Since the beginning of the project in 1996, the LWP team has collected approximately 2000 interactions, ranging from large meetings to small meetings, from two day planning meetings to short brainstorming meetings, encompassing social talk at work breaks, and even telephone conversations, involving in total over 700 people in more than 30 different New Zealand workplaces. Our first recordings were undertaken in four different New Zealand government departments. A number of volunteers in each workplace audio recorded small meetings, telephone calls, and even morning and afternoon teas. Participants included people working in a number of different jobs and at different levels. Administration staff, policy analysts and managers were all included, and the data highlighted the importance of relational (e.g. small talk) as well as transactional (task-related) aspects of talk at work (Holmes and Stubbe 2003).

In the next phase of data collection, we recorded a set of larger meetings from mainly commercial organisations. For these meetings we used video cameras fixed in position in the meeting rooms and since we started the recording before people entered we were able to capture the small talk as well as the more formal meeting interaction. Six New Zealand workplaces recorded team meetings, while three of the workplaces also recorded a number of smaller meetings. Meeting processes and leadership styles were major themes that emerged from this dataset (Marra 2003; Schnurr et al. 2007; Schnurr 2009).

In order to explore leadership issues more fully, along with the relationship between leadership, ethnicity and language use, our next dataset was collected in two Māori workplaces which were each paired with a Pākehā workplace within the same industry (Holmes et al. 2011). Māori are the indigenous people of New Zealand; Pākehā are the colonisers, with roots mainly in Britain. This data collection involved considerable negotiation to take account of acceptable ways of working with Māori people (see Smith 1999; Holmes et al. 2011, chapter 2). Managers in each of the four workplaces recorded one-to-one and larger meetings, providing data which allowed exploration of the way they enacted leadership in a range of contexts. A pilot for this leadership project was also undertaken with a leader in a bi-cultural organisation, data from which is discussed below. In this enterprise we also engaged in a very fruitful interdisciplinary partnership with leadership and management experts. For example, Brad Jackson, then Director of the Centre for the Study of Leadership at Victoria University of Wellington, interviewed the male leaders about their approach to leadership (Vine et al. 2008). Working with Professor Jackson and his team provided some interesting challenges in relation to unrecognised theoretical and methodological assumptions on both sides. However this interdisciplinary work proved very rewarding in terms of new insights and applications.

More recently, professional migrants and their acquisition of and adaptation to New Zealand ways of interacting became an important focus of our research (e.g. Holmes, Joe et al. 2011; Holmes and Riddiford 2011; Riddiford and Holmes 2015). Pragmatics can be a difficult aspect of a language for non-native speakers and lack of proficiency in this area can affect their ability to find work. Previous research has found that this is an aspect of learning to communicate in another language as an adult that needs to be explicitly taught (Pearson 2010). A group of skilled migrants allowed us to follow their progress as they completed a course at Victoria University of Wellington aimed at helping them develop their awareness and use of pragmatics in New Zealand business contexts. This included recording role-plays and interviews as part of their coursework, as well as following them as they undertook internships in Wellington businesses (Riddiford and Joe 2010). We were not only able to demonstrate to them the benefit of being involved in the research, but also the ways their involvement with our research could benefit others in similar situations (https://worktalk.immigration.govt.nz/index.html).

The workplaces outlined so far are all white-collar professional workplaces and the recordings typically took place in offices and meeting rooms within each organisation. The LWP has also gathered data from other types of workplaces, for instance, recording data from nurses working on a hospital ward. This context involved not only recordings of nurses with their colleagues, but also between nurses and patients, adding an interesting dimension to many of the interactions (Holmes and Major 2003; Major and Holmes 2008). Blue-collar workplaces have also been included in our research with data from factories (Holmes and Stubbe 2003; Stubbe 2010), and retail outlets (Holmes and Fillary 2000). The factory environment provides many challenges to data collection, such as considerable noise, the brief nature of many interactions, and the mobility of participants. These factors also have consequences for the way communication occurs: directives, for instance, tend to be expressed quickly and directly, without time for the explanations and discussion which characterise directives in white-collar contexts (Vine 2004, 2020, chapter 3).

Some of the challenges to data collection in a factory environment also proved relevant in data collection on construction sites (Holmes and

Woodhams 2013; Holmes and Marra 2017) and in eldercare facilities (Marsden and Holmes 2014; Vine et al. 2021). Equipment such as skill saws and other power tools make construction sites a noisy place in which to record. Participants are also very active and are often very focused on completing a task so talk may be sporadic. Recording in eldercare sites involved caregivers who were moving from one room to another, with televisions or radios often playing loudly in the background. Using armbands in which to locate the recorders in these environments kept the recorders as mobile as the participants, enabling them to carry on their work as usual while also ensuring the participants' data was audible.

The most recent data collection we have undertaken has involved service encounters in shops and in a museum (Vine and Marra 2017; Marra et al. forthcoming). A new approach was needed when collecting this data, with a "mystery shopper" technique being adopted. This entailed researchers carrying non-conspicuous recorders and recording over an agreed time period. The workers in this case knew they could be recorded for the project, but did not know specifically when this would occur. This was a way of managing another challenging type of workplace environment where members of the public could not ethically be recorded, so we became the customers or visitors requesting services.

Our data collection has thus encompassed a diverse range of workplaces, from international commercial organisations, through government departments to factories, building sites and shops. Each type of workplace has presented challenges for data collection and we have adapted our methodology in order to respond to these challenges and continue to gather good quality interactional data.

Participants have ranged from company Chief Executive Officers to administration staff, building and site foremen to apprentices, factory line workers and museum hosts. The people who have recorded their daily interactions for us have been at many different stages in their working lives, some still learning aspects of their jobs, some well-established, while others are looking forward to retirement. Some workplaces have an even gender balance, while others are predominantly female or male. Participants have also come from a broad range of ethnic backgrounds. New Zealand's workforce is diverse and this is reflected in the backgrounds of the people who have been involved with our project.

Theoretical Framework

Our approach to analysing workplace discourse has its roots in interactional sociolinguistics (Gumperz 1999; Gordon and Kraut 2018), an approach which analyses discourse in its wider socio-cultural context and draws on the analysts' knowledge of the community and its norms in interpreting what is going on in an interaction. As illustrated below, we identify features of discourse that index a range of different kinds of contextual information, such as age or ethnicity, or stances such as aggressive, collaborative, deferential, or collegial, associated with particular social groups (e.g. Schiffrin 2003). The goal is to explore how social meaning is discursively conveyed and inferred in particular interactions, and researchers typically bring detailed knowledge of the specific social context to the analysis, often based on extensive ethnographic observations, as reflected in our methodology.

Interactional sociolinguistics is especially concerned to investigate linguistic and cultural diversity. If the people interacting do not share or recognise each other's interactional norms, this can lead to misunderstandings. Misunderstandings can have damaging social consequences, particularly for those from minority groups. An interactional sociolinguistics approach can therefore help identify where norms may differ. This is therefore an approach where the *relevance* of the research being undertaken is an important basic consideration.

We combine interactional sociolinguistics with a social constructionist framework, examining how social meanings are expressed in workplace relationships, and how social identities are negotiated and maintained through talk. Interaction and identity construction are conceptualised as dynamic processes where meanings and intentions are jointly and progressively negotiated between the individuals involved. This approach emphasises the constantly changing and developing nature of social identities, social categories and group boundaries, a process in which talk clearly plays an essential part (e.g. Blommaert 2007; Cameron 2009). A social constructionist approach within an interactional sociolinguistic framework provides a productive means of analysing how people enact, reflect, and reinforce their workplace identities through their talk at work.

As noted above, we also draw on a range of background and self-reported information to support our detailed discourse analyses and interpretations of talk in action.

In sum, we analyse authentic everyday workplace talk for evidence of the way people negotiate social relationships at work, as well as how they discursively construct different facets of their social identities, examining both what they say and how they say it. The focus is typically on successful communication, and how people manage to both establish rapport and achieve their transactional goals through effective workplace talk. The analysis involves paying particular attention to the clues people use to interpret conversational interaction within its ethnographic context. This ranges from considerations of content, narrative structure, small talk, humour, and turn-taking patterns to detailed analysis of pronoun use, discourse markers (e.g. *oh*, *okay*, *well*), pauses, hesitations, and paralinguistic behaviour, as well as other relevant discourse features. We illustrate some of these features in the following section by discussing six excerpts from a workplace meeting, in which a respected and effective leader demonstrates his particular style of management.

Analysis of Workplace Discourse

Meetings are widely regarded as the very stuff of work, especially in white-collar professional contexts. As noted in our earlier work (Holmes and Stubbe 2003), they provide opportunities both for the expression of institutional power and authority relationships, as well as a range of aspects of rapport management (Spencer-Oatey 2008). They also provide opportunities for identity construction, and the excerpts below demonstrate how analysis of data from authentic workplace interaction provides insights regarding how a manager, Greg,[2] constructs a range of facets of his social identity, including his identity as a professional, a considerate manager, and an expert in Māori language.

Greg structures his team meetings with a formal opening section which includes a Māori component, followed by consultation on all agenda items including extensive discussion, and concluding with a relaxed ending in which after his brief closing utterance, *okay thank you very much*, work talk segues into social talk. The opening is particularly interesting as Greg uses it as an opportunity to teach his team (who do not know much Māori) the meaning of a *whakataukī* or Māori proverb. We have analysed many meetings in Māori workplaces (see, for example, Holmes and Marra 2011), and the standard meeting opening is a *karakia*, a prayer, or recitation in Māori by the meeting chair. Greg chooses to use something slightly different here, and he has designated Marama to read the proverb.

Example 1

[The italicised words cite the proverb being discussed]

1. Greg:	well kia ora tātou [translation: greetings everyone]
2.	and welcome back Susie
3. Susie:	thank you ...
4. Greg:	so um +++ we'll start with our whakataukī
5. Marama:	okay + *mātua whakapai i tōu marae*
6.	*ka whakapai ai i te marae o te tangata* [translation: put your own house/marae in order first before you presume to improve someone else's]
7. Kendra:	[laughs]: mm:
8. All:	*mātua whakapai i tōu marae*
9.	*ka whakapai ai i te marae o te tangata*
10. Blake:	help
11. Marama:	*mātua* does that mean first
12.	//of all? mm\
13. Greg:	/first yeah yeah\\ it's an interesting word ... [Greg goes on to discuss the meaning of *mātua* and the proverb as a whole]

The *whakataukī* serves not just as a formal means of opening the meeting, but also as a way of promoting thinking about Māori values. The standard response to *karakia* in our dataset used to open meetings is to respond *amene* (amen) or to remain silent, before the chair then introduces the agenda for the meeting. Here we see a very different response, reflecting Greg's goal of promoting discussion and thinking about the meaning of the proverb. First Kendra laughs (line 7), perhaps indicating that she regards the translation task as a difficult one—laughter is a common response to a difficult demand (Glenn 2003). Blake is quite explicitly confounded, as his low-pitched response *help* (line 10) indicates, while Marama begins the discussion process by asking about the meaning of the word *mātua* (line 11). Greg's practice here illustrates some distinctive features of his leadership style: he is concerned to encourage learning among his team members, while also enacting his Māori identity.

Greg also displays his expertise in the Māori language, a highly valued skill in this government workplace committed to improving educational outcomes for all New Zealanders, and a skill which is relatively rare in New Zealand as a whole. The Māori language is significantly endangered, and Māori adults with Greg's proficiency in the language number only 11% (Statistics New Zealand 2013). There is clear evidence in the data, however, that in line with Māori beliefs which value humility and modesty—captured in the concept of *whakaiti* 'being humble, modest' (Metge 1995)—alongside the general New Zealand preference for avoiding boasting, or sticking one's head above the parapet (Holmes et al. 2009; Jackson and Parry 2001; Holmes et al. 2017), and the high value placed by Māori on *whakaiti* or modesty, Greg does not present himself as a self-promoting leader. So, for example, instead of delivering the *whakataukī* himself, Marama presents it. Moreover, when she asks about the meaning of the word *mātua,* he responds with an explanation, but rather than claiming expert status for this knowledge, he qualifies his explanation with an account of how he came to understand this particular meaning of the word.

Example 2

1. Marama:	*mātua* does that mean first
2.	//of all? mm\
3. Greg:	/first yeah yeah\\ it's an interesting word it
4.	y- yeah you say *me mātua mōhio*
	[translation: you you sh- you need to know this first]
	//it's um\
5. Marama:	/mm\\
6. Greg:	it's um + er and it's not actually a very common word

7.	//but + I seemed to hear it\ a lot in [tribe]
8. Marama:	/no I didn't know it I was quite surprised\\
9. Greg:	well [name] used to use it all the time
10.	that's why I actually know the word //[laughs]\
11. Marama:	/oh okay\\

The most widely known and frequently used meaning of the word *mātua* is parents (or relatives of older generation) (Williams 1971), but here, as Greg explains, the meaning is different; it means 'first' or 'foremost'. He expands its meaning as *you need to know this first* (line 4), acknowledging that this meaning is not common (line 6), and explaining that he learned it in the context of its use by a member of a specific tribe (line 7), who *used to use it all the time* (line 9). Marama responds by confirming her lack of familiarity with this meaning *I didn't know it I was quite surprised* (line 8), and her appreciation of Greg's explanation of why he knows this meaning, *oh okay* (line 11). Greg's position here is totally consistent with the stance taken by other Māori leaders we have worked with (Holmes et al. 2011). He adopts a modest stance, indexing an ethnically appropriate leadership identity, consistent with Māori values such as *whakaiti.*

In terms of achieving the transactional goals of the organisation, Greg is a very consultative leader, seeking the opinions of others rather than laying down the law or wading in first with his own views. Unlike many authoritative and masculinist leaders (Baxter 2010), Greg does not dominate the talk; he listens most of the time, and rarely contributes at length. His style is characterised by pragmatic devices which attenuate and hedge statements of his opinion (hedges are in italics):

e.g.

1. and it's *sort of like I think* we need a discussion at the m g [management group] about what *if anything* we do next
2. *you know* it's getting *a bit* [voc] legs of its own here and um

He favours sociopragmatic strategies which involve indirect and inclusive ways of indicating what he wants done (e.g. using the pronouns *we* and *us*), and he often explicitly seeks advice:

e.g.

1. we need to look at the context
2. I need some guidance about how far we go with this because *um you know* we need [voc] getting all the stuff together

After laying out an issue for discussion, for instance, he asks *so what are we gonna do then?*, and he proceeds to allow all team members to voice their views before beginning to seek consensus. Example 3 illustrates how Greg manages another discussion regarding membership of a particular committee. Once again he begins by asking his team, *so what are we gonna do then?* Blake has suggested that one of Theo's team be invited to join the committee.

Example 3

1. Greg:	so what are we gonna do then?
2. Theo:	I guess I guess I should have the first say
3.	seeing (he's) my staff member and I would support it
4. Marama:	mm
5. Aroha:	I think it's a good idea too +
6. Greg:	yep + Kendra?
7. Kendra:	mm
8. Blake:	Susie's looking sad there //why ( ) [laughs]\
9. Susie:	/no not at all I'm just\\
10.	I just I don't feel I've got a um particular opinion on it
11.	I haven't got a handle on it really about what
12.	I mean I d- I don't see any reason why not
13.	although I just wondered about it becoming quite a big committee
14.	that was all
15. Greg:	[reassuring tone]: it's just //the same size:\
16. Aroha:	/it's quite small\\
17. Blake:	it's still quite small
18. Susie:	oh well that's alright then
19. Blake:	it's um //one\ two three four five six
20. Greg:	/alright\\
	[Greg proceeds to sum up the agreed position]

It is noticeable that Greg allows every person present to voice an opinion and does not participate, except to join with others in reassuring Susie that the committee is not an unusually large one. Once a consensus has been reached he closes the discussion on that issue *alright,* and sums up. Many other chairs whose discourse we have analysed take a much more active role in ensuring the decision reached is one they want (Marra 2003; Holmes et al. 2011; Holmes and Chiles 2009).

As a leader, Greg is particularly skilled at managing the relational dimensions of interaction. Relational work refers very broadly to all the ways in which people attend to the face needs of others. It is "the 'work' individuals invest in negotiating relationships with others" (Locher and Watts 2005, p. 10). Greg attends to the face needs of others with sensitivity and actively contributes to building rapport and solidarity between team members. This is evident in a range of ways: he is responsive to the opinions of others, providing consistent verbal and non-verbal feedback; he expresses approval for suggestions; and he uses the Māori phrase *ka pai,* 'good', frequently throughout the meeting. He also uses a good deal of humour, thus contributing to a positive atmosphere and providing a regular welcome break in the serious discussions. He jokes, for example, regarding some lost papers from an overseas department, *don't they have carrier pigeon?* Example 4 is a typical instance of Greg providing appreciation and positive feedback to his team members.

Example 4

1. Greg::	um thanks everybody for the hel- support that they gave um Kendra
2.	and Tom for the select committee um
3.	and I've [voc] it went really well I was really pleased with it
4.	and I mean but but everyb-
5.	but people like Josephine and Wendy just dropped tools
6.	and got stuff yeah and in a few minutes
7.	and even John Evans he + rattled rattled up something
8.	you know ...

9.	and Kendra that that that little speech
10.	that you gave me was really good to have too

Finally, Greg participates fully in the small talk of his team members, not only at the beginning and end of the meetings, but also at regular points during the meetings. The team often digresses into what seems very personal social talk but, as in other Māori meetings we have analysed (Holmes et al. 2011), the apparent digression often serves a useful informative function too.

Example 5

1. Kendra:	anyway just an update on Reg
2.	as you know he's been buying a house
3.	he's bought a house
4.	and now he's sold his own one all //very quickly\
5. Blake:	/already?\\
6. Kendra:	yes //and it's all brilliant\
7. Susie:	/in Napier\\ (all) Napier
8. Kendra:	yes that's right so he probably will be less distracted
9.	when he returns this week
10. Blake:	[laughs]

Kendra is here providing what could be considered 'gossip' about Reg in relation to house buying and selling. But she is also doing relevant relational work since Reg is a member of the team. The information she provides is presented as an 'account', explaining the fact that he has been *distracted* (line 8) during the last few weeks. The responses indicate that people are pleased to hear Reg's good news.

So Kendra's social talk makes a double contribution to the rapport building in the team; she provides input to the ongoing social talk while also doing relational work for Reg in relation to his apparent lack of orientation to work in the last little while. It is often the case, as here, especially in meetings we have analysed in Māori workplaces (Holmes et al. 2011; Kell et al. 2007) that a contribution which initially or superficially appears to be purely social small talk also provides information relevant to the workplace's transactional goals. The double function of Kendra's contribution is very clear; other examples we have analysed are often subtle and opaque to those outside the specific community of practice concerned. Triangulation in the form of post-recording interviews, together with an understanding of the cultural context, are obviously valuable in such cases to assist with interpretation and analysis.

In his contributions to the team's small talk, Greg also shares personal information, in this way building close and trusting relationships between team members. At various points, he talks about his children, his brother, and his father. In the following example, he explains why he is picking his brother up from the airport and driving him to the town of Masterton where he (Greg) will also visit a work site.

Example 6

1. Greg:	cos my father can't drive now
2.	cos er he does drive I'm just sh- t- I'm
3.	but he's blind and he drives the bloody car
4.	//and I said you ++\
5.	/[general laughter]\\
6. Greg	he has like a magnifying glass to read the paper
7. Kendra:	[laughs]
8. Marama:	and he drives the //(car)\
9. Greg:	/and he\\ said I'm worried that I won't get my licence +
10.	you know when he turns eighty
11.	you gotta go for another driver's licence //(which is)\
12. Theo:	/are you worried\\ that he will?
13. Susie:	that's been //wiped out now\
14. Greg:	/[laughs]: I worry:\\
15.	[general laughter throughout next section]
16. Kendra:	I think that's wiped
17. Marsha:	that's wiped now
18. Kendra:	that's quite a worry
19. Greg:	yeah anyway

Again the contribution serves the purpose not only of sharing personal information and building rapport, but also informs his team about Greg's whereabouts and activities. Moreover, this example illustrates very nicely the good relationship between the team members. They all jointly contribute to this exchange, laughing appreciatively at Greg's story about his father's 'unfittedness' for driving. The friendly relationship is also indicated by Greg's use of a very informal style, signalled by exaggeration *but he's blind* (line 3) and the use of a swear word *he drives the bloody car* (line 3). Theo's response to Greg's report of his father's fear that he might not get another licence *are you worried that he will?* (line 12) is made in a jocular tone. There is a great deal of overlapping talk and laughter as the team members develop a shared floor with various contributions: Marsha and Kendra comment that the requirement for another driving test at age eighty has been *wiped out* (lines 13, 16–17) and Kendra's response *that's quite a worry* (line 18) may be a comment on Greg's father's driving capacity or on the abolition of the test requirement. This is typical collaborative friendly talk between people who get on well.

We have illustrated in this section how discourse analysis of authentic workplace interaction can throw light on the ways in which people use language at work, not only to accomplish their transactional goals, getting the work done through strategic planning and decision-making, but also maintaining and developing good workplace relationships through other-oriented collaborative talk and humour. It is clear that Greg enacts a distinctive relationally-oriented leadership style as well as indexing his Māori identity throughout workplace interactions with his team members. The importance of understanding the specific context when examining data has also been highlighted. In the final section, we discuss some of the ways in which our analyses have been put to use, with the aim of contributing to more effective communication in the real world of work.

Applications: Workshops and Teaching Materials

At every point in our LWP research, a priority has been to make the findings of our research relevant to workplaces. Initially, this involved presenting interactive workshops and providing written reports to organisations participating in our research (see Vine 2016). But we have also developed some very practical ways of making our analyses more widely useful. It is important to emphasize that our goals are never prescriptive. We aim to equip students and workplace participants with the skills required to undertake their own sociopragmatic analysis, and thus to determine for themselves an appropriate way of presenting themselves in the range of specific situations they encounter. Here we briefly outline five cases where a practical application has extended beyond the immediate workplace in which the data was collected (see Vine 2016 and Vine and Marra 2017 for summaries of some other applications).

A collaborative project with staff at the Eastern Institute of Technology (EIT) on the east coast of the North Island of New Zealand aimed to help students with intellectual disabilities integrate into a new workplace. These students were completing a work and life skills course through the institute. We recorded data in a range of different workplaces, and the analysis, undertaken with Rose Fillary, a teacher on the course, highlighted a number of areas where the students were doing very well, but also areas where teaching and preparation of the students for entering a workplace could be enhanced. Insights from these findings were published in journals for teachers/trainers, providing the potential for the findings to be applied to other programmes (Holmes and Fillary 2000).

More recently, naturally occurring data from eldercare facilities and construction sites has provided direct input into teaching resources developed for teaching refugees and migrants to New Zealand who are aiming to find work in these industries. Small interactive episodes were identified which illustrate a number of communication issues which could cause problems for non-native speakers. These were re-recorded by Nicky Riddiford using native speaking volunteers and used as the basis of lessons which highlight specific vocabulary and interaction patterns. The original recordings could not be used due to confidentiality agreements; moreover the unedited transcripts were too challenging for learners with limited proficiency in English. However, the interactive patterns and the range of topics identified in the original recordings which were based on authentic interaction provided sufficiently rich teaching materials in the opinion of the ESL experts to justify this process. No other such materials existed based on genuine interactions in the types of workplaces where the refugees and migrants hoped to obtain employment. Topics covered include understanding directives and giving instructions appropriately. The resources, produced by experienced ESL teachers and researchers (Nicky Riddiford and Judi McCallum), are available for free download through the LWP website (www.victoria.ac.nz/lals/centres-and-institutes/language-in-the-workplace/resources/teaching-and-learning-resources).

These two examples involve providing resources for teachers working with students who want to work in blue-collar workplaces. Data collected and analysed by the project team over the years from white-collar workplaces has also been used as input for teaching resources for professional migrants. Victoria University of Wellington's Workplace Communication for Skilled Migrants programme, which has been running since 2005, uses excerpts from the LWP data to illustrate how native speakers interact in New Zealand workplaces (see Prebble 2007). Analysing authentic examples has proved invaluable in helping students develop their pragmatic skills (Holmes, Joe et al. 2011; Holmes and Riddiford 2011). Rather than providing formulaic responses for a necessarily limited range of contexts, the course focusses on assisting students to analyse the examples in order to identify the critical social relationships and contextual factors, thus equipping them to cope in a wide range of real-life workplace interactions. The materials produced for the course have also been compiled into a course book, making them available to other teachers (Riddiford and Newton 2010).

Enhancing communication between native speakers is also an important issue for professional white-collar workplaces and was the motivation for the Communication Evaluation and Development (CED) model which was developed by members of the LWP team (Jones and Stubbe

2004). Bringing together expertise in both sociolinguistics and organisational communication, this model provides a tool which can be used by organisations to improve communication. Adopting an action research approach, employees are encouraged to examine and evaluate their own communication, learning to observe and reflect on their interactions with others at work. Utilising insights from our research on effective communication at work, they are then able to plan and modify aspects of their communication which they consider problematic.

A final case draws on data from throughout the life of the project, as well as from research on authentic workplace data conducted around the world. Vine (2020) is an introductory textbook not only for linguistics students, but also for those studying workplace discourse from a business communication or management perspective. It assumes no prior background in linguistics. Example 3 above, from Greg and his team, is included in order to illustrate both what a more hands-off approach to leadership can look like (Vine 2020, pp. 177–178), as well as the way that people can modify the way they interact given the gender mix of their audience (Vine 2020, pp. 192–193). The men take consultative stances in this extract and both women and men use hedges, attenuating their opinions, and pay attention to interpersonal aspects of the interaction. Both the women and the men use language that is associated with more feminine styles of speech. In the textbook, this interactional style is contrasted with examples of Theo and Blake interacting one-on-one with Greg, where their language is often more direct. The material and discussion in the textbook demonstrates an approach where the way the analysis is presented and the aspects foregrounded are tailored to the audience and the research questions being addressed. Articles in academic journals and scholarly books require a higher level of detail and typically entail more technical analysis and specialised linguistic jargon. Our commitment to providing materials and discussion which is accessible to a range of different types of audiences, however, is important in achieving our goal of applying our research in the real world.

Conclusion

In this chapter, we have presented a case study of a large project which over more than twenty years has been collecting and analysing data from a range of different types of workplaces in New Zealand. Authenticity, triangulation, background and relevance are four issues that have been at the centre of our approach to collecting, analysing and reporting on the findings of our research.

Gaining access to workplaces is an important and often unreported aspect of data collection which is not always easy, and we began by highlighting how we tackled this issue. Each setting where data has been recorded has presented different challenges (Vine and Marra 2017), but adapting and collaborating with people in each workplace has produced a rich database of authentic interactions which have formed the basis for numerous research articles, as well as resources aimed at helping people communicate more effectively at work.

Basing research on authentic talk produces a much richer appreciation of workplace communication than using staged interactions or just interviewing people about their communication practices. What people *think* they do and what they *actually* do can be quite different. People also often fail to realise the importance of everyday talk to their success in the workplace and to the success of organisations (Vine 2020, chapter 9).

The aspects of language and the issues we have examined have varied over the years, often defined and refined in consultation with members of the organisations with whom we have worked (see Holmes and Stubbe 2003; Holmes et al. 2011, p. 32). With a focus on successful communication, we have also been able to provide input to the workplaces we have worked with, highlighting what they do well. Discussing our results with them has deepened our understanding of workplace talk in New Zealand, and in their feedback workplace participants involved in the research have emphasised the positive impact of working with us on their own communication practices, together with increased awareness of the importance of how they communicate.

Research in language studies increasingly involves interdisciplinary cooperation. This is undoubtedly challenging, as our own experiences working with experts in management and leadership testifies. In every case, we needed to devote a good deal of time to clarifying terminology, defining crucial concepts in each of the contributing disciplines, and negotiating what could be taken for granted versus what needed to be made explicit in our joint analyses. Both sides have had important contributions to make, with sociolinguistics providing tools for engaging meaningfully with the more recent recognition of the importance of language in leadership (e.g. Fairhurst 2007). The pay-off of joint work in this area was a richer and more nuanced analysis and understanding of workplace interaction with a wider range of potential real world applications.

Transcription Conventions

... //...\	simultaneous or overlapping utterance of 'first' speaker
/...\\ ...	simultaneous or overlapping utterance of 'second' speaker
[laughs]	paralinguistic features and editorial comments in square brackets, colons indicate start/finish
[voc]	vocalisation
...	omitted section of transcript
un-	cut off word, both self and other interruption
( )	untranscribable or incomprehensible speech
(well)	transcriber's best guess at unclear speech
+	pause of up to one second
++	one- to two-second pause
+++	two- to three-second pause

Notes

1. We would like to acknowledge a range of sources of funding for our project over many years, initially from the New Zealand Foundation for Research, Science and Technology, and then from the Royal Society of New Zealand through a Marsden Grant, and from government departments including the Settlement Division of the Department of Labour and the Ministry of Business, Innovation and Employment. Throughout

this period we have received financial assistance from the Victoria University Research Fund and Faculty of Humanities and Social Sciences Research Fund to support our research when external funding was not available.

2. All names are pseudonyms.

References

Baxter, J. (2010). *The language of female leadership*. London: Palgrave Macmillan.

Blommaert, J. (2007). Sociolinguistics and discourse analysis: Orders of indexicality and polycentricity. *Journal of Multicultural Discourses, 2*, 115–130.

Cameron, D. (2009). Theoretical issues for the study of gender and spoken interaction. In P. Pichler & E. M. Eppler (Eds.), *Gender and spoken interaction* (pp. 1–17). London: Palgrave Macmillan.

Cooperrider, D. L., Whitney, D., & Stavros, J. M. (2003). *Appreciative inquiry handbook*. Bedford Heights, OH: Lakeshore Publishers.

Drew, P., & Heritage, J. (Eds.). (1992). *Talk at work: Interaction in institutional settings*. Cambridge: Cambridge University Press.

Fairhurst, G. (2007). *Discursive leadership*. London: Sage.

Glenn, P. (2003). *Laughter in interaction*. Cambridge: Cambridge University Press.

Gordon, C., & Kraut, J. (2018). Interactional sociolinguistics. In B. Vine (Ed.), *The Routledge handbook of language in the workplace* (pp. 3–14). Abingdon: Routledge.

Gumperz, J. (1999). On interactional sociolinguistic method. In S. Sarangi & C. Roberts (Eds.), *Talk, work and institutional order. Discourse in medical, mediation and management settings* (pp. 453–471). Berlin/New York: Mouton de Gruyter.

Hodgkinson, G. P., & Rousseau, D. M. (2009). Bridging the rigour–relevance gap in management research: It's already happening! *Journal of Management Studies, 46*, 534–546.

Holmes, J. (2000a). Politeness, power and provocation: How humour functions in the workplace. *Discourse Studies, 2*, 159–185.

Holmes, J. (2000b). Doing collegiality and keeping control at work: Small talk in government departments. In J. Coupland (Ed.), *Small talk* (pp. 32–61). London: Longman.

Holmes, J. (2000c). Women at work: Analysing women's talk in New Zealand workplaces. *Australian Review of Applied Linguistics (ARAL), 22*, 1–17.

Holmes, J. (2005). When small talk is a big deal: Sociolinguistic challenges in the workplace. In M. H. Long (Ed.), *Second language needs analysis* (pp. 344–371). Cambridge University Press.

Holmes, J. (2019). Researching the impact of 'the culture order' in professional workplace contexts. In K. Hyland & L. Wong (Eds.), *Specialised English: New directions in ESP and EAP research and practice* (pp. 135–148). London: Routledge.

Holmes, J., Bell, A., & Boyce, M. (1991). Variation and change in New Zealand English: A social dialect investigation (Project report for the Foundation of Research, Science and Technology). Wellington, Victoria University, Linguistics Department.

Holmes, J., & Chiles, T. (2009). "Is that right?" questions and questioning as control devices in the workplace. In A. F. Freed & S. Ehrlich (Eds.), *Why do you ask?: The 7 functions of questions in institutional discourse* (pp. 187–210). New York: Oxford University Press.

Holmes, J., & Fillary, R. (2000). Handling small talk at work: Challenges for workers with intellectual disabilities. *International Journal of Disability, Development and Education, 47*, 273–291.

Holmes, J., Joe, A., Marra, M., Newton, J., Riddiford, N., & Vine, B. (2011a). Applying linguistic research to real world problems: The case of the Wellington Language in the Workplace Project. In C. Candlin & S. Sarangi (Eds.), *Handbook of communication in organisations and professions* (pp. 533–549). Berlin: Mouton de Gruyter.

Holmes, J., & Major, G. (2003). Talking to patients: The complexity of communication on the ward. *Vision—A Journal of Nursing, 11*, 4–9.

Holmes, J., & Marra, M. (2002). Having a laugh at work: How humour contributes to workplace culture. *Journal of Pragmatics, 34*, 1683–1710.

Holmes, J., & Marra, M. (2011). Relativity rules: Politic talk in ethnicised workplaces. In B. L. Davies, M. Haugh, & A. J. Merrison (Eds.), *Situated politeness* (pp. 27–52). London: Continuum.

Holmes, J., & Marra, M. (2017). "You're a proper tradesman mate": Constructing a professional identity in construction. In D. Van De Mieroop & S. Schnurr (Eds.), *Identity struggles. Evidence from workplaces around the world* (pp. 127–145). Amsterdam: John Benjamins.

Holmes, J., Marra, M., & Lazzaro-Salazar, M. (2017). Negotiating the tall poppy syndrome in New Zealand workplaces: Women leaders managing the challenge. *Gender and Language, 11*, 1–29.

Holmes, J., Marra, M., & Vine, B. (2011b). *Leadership, discourse and ethnicity*. Oxford: Oxford University Press.

Holmes, J., & Riddiford, N. (2011). From classroom to workplace: Tracking socio-pragmatic development. *ELT Journal, 65*, 376–386.

Holmes, J., & Stubbe, M. (2003). *Power and politeness in the workplace*. London: Pearson. [Re-issued as 2nd edition with new Preface by Routledge 2015].

Holmes, J., Stubbe, M., & Vine, B. (1999). Constructing professional identity: "Doing power" in policy units. In S. Sarangi & C. Roberts (Eds.), *Talk, work and institutional order. Discourse in medical, mediation and management settings* (pp. 351–385). Berlin/New York: Mouton de Gruyter.

Holmes, J., Vine, B., & Johnson, G. (1998). *Guide to the Wellington corpus of spoken New Zealand English*. Wellington, New Zealand: School of Linguistics and Applied Language Studies, Victoria University of Wellington.

Holmes, J., Vine, B., & Marra, M. (2009). Māori men at work: Leadership discourse and ethnic identity. *Intercultural Pragmatics, 6*, 345–366.

Holmes, J., & Woodhams, J. (2013). Building interaction: The role of talk in joining a community of practice. *Discourse and Communication, 7*, 276–298.

Jackson, B., & Parry, K. (2001). *The hero manager: Learning from New Zealand's top chief executives*. Auckland, NZ: Penguin.

Jones, D., & Stubbe, M. (2004). Communication and the reflective practitioner: A shared perspective from sociolinguistics and organisational communication. *International Journal of Applied Linguistics, 14*, 185–211.

Karinthy, F. (1929). Chain-links (Láncszemek). Retrieved from https://djjr-courses.wdfiles.com/local%2D%2Dfiles/soc180%3Akarinthy-chain-links/Karinthy-Chain-Links_1929.pdf

Kell, S., Marra, M., Holmes, J., & Vine, B. (2007). Ethnic differences in the dynamics of women's work meetings. *Multilingua, 26*, 309–331.

Kieser, A., & Leiner, L. (2009). Why the rigour–relevance gap in management research is unbridgeable. *Journal of Management Studies, 4*, 516–533.

Labov, W. (1972). *Sociolinguistic patterns*. Philadelphia: University of Pennsylvania.

Locher, M., & Watts, R. J. (2005). Politeness theory and relational work. *Journal of Politeness Research, 1*, 9–34.

Major, G., & Holmes, J. (2008). How do nurses describe health care procedures? Analysing nurse-patient interaction in a hospital ward. *Australian Journal of Advanced Nursing, 25*, 58–70.

Marra, M. (2003). *Decisions in New Zealand business meetings: A sociolinguistic analysis of power at work*. PhD thesis, Victoria University of Wellington.

Marra, M., Holmes, J., & Vine, B. (Forthcoming). What we share: The impact of norms on successful interaction. To appear in J. Mortensen & K. Kraft (Eds.). *Norms and the Study of Language in Social Life*. Berlin: Mouton de Gruyter.

Marsden, S., & Holmes, J. (2014). Talking to the elderly in New Zealand residential care settings. *Journal of Pragmatics, 64*, 17–34.

Metge, J. (1995). *New growth from old: The whanau in the modern world.* Wellington, NZ: Victoria University Press.

Pearson, L. (2010). Preface. In A. Martinez-Flor & E. Uso-Juan (Eds.), *Speech act performance: Theoretical, empirical and methodological issues* (pp. xiii–xiv). Amsterdam: John Benjamins.

Prebble, J. (2007). *Workplace communication for skilled migrants: English for Professional Purposes VUW ELIN941*. Language in the Workplace Occasional Papers 6.

Riddiford, N., & Holmes, J. (2015). Assisting the development of sociopragmatic skills: Negotiating refusals at work. *System, 48*, 129–140.

Riddiford, N., & Joe, A. (2010). Tracking the development of sociopragmatic skills. *TESOL Quarterly, 44*, 195–205.

Riddiford, N., & Newton, J. (2010). *Workplace talk in action—An ESOL resource*. Wellington: School of Linguistics and Applied Language Studies, Victoria University of Wellington.

Schiffrin, D. (2003). Discourse markers: Language, meaning and context. In D. Schiffrin, D. Tannen, & H. E. Hamilton (Eds.), *The handbook of discourse analysis* (pp. 54–57). Oxford: Blackwell.

Schnurr, S. (2009). *Leadership discourse at work: Interactions of humour, gender and workplace culture*. Basingstoke/New York: Palgrave Macmillan.

Schnurr, S., Marra, M., & Holmes, J. (2007). Leadership and communication: Discursive evidence of a workplace culture change. *Discourse and Communication, 1*, 433–451.

Smith, L. T. (1999). *Decolonizing methodologies: Research and indigenous peoples.* Dunedin: University of Otago Press.

Spencer-Oatey, H. (2008). *Culturally speaking: Managing rapport through talk across cultures* (2nd ed.). London: Continuum.

Statistics New Zealand. (2013). *Te Kupenga 2013 (Survey of Māori well-being).* Retrieved from https://www.stats.govt.nz/information-releases/te-kupenga-2013-english

Stubbe, M. (2010). *"Was that my misunderstanding?": Managing miscommunication and problematic talk at work.* PhD thesis, Victoria University of Wellington.

Vine, B. (2004). *Getting things done at work: The discourse of power in workplace interaction.* Amsterdam/Philadelphia: John Benjamins.

Vine, B. (2016). The Wellington language in the workplace project: Engaging with the research and wider communities. In A. Mearns & K. P. Corrigan (Eds.), *Creating and digitizing language corpora: Vol. 3: Databases for public engagement* (pp. 321–346). Basingstoke: Palgrave Macmillan.

Vine, B. (2020). *Introducing language in the workplace.* Cambridge: Cambridge University Press.

Vine, B., Holmes, J., Marra, M., Pfeifer, D., & Jackson, B. (2008). Exploring co-leadership talk through interactional sociolinguistics. *Leadership, 4*, 339–360.

Vine, B., Kell, S., Marra, M., & Holmes, J. (2009). Boundary marking humour: Institutional gender and ethnic demarcation. In N. R. Norrick & D. Chiaro (Eds.), *Humor in interaction* (pp. 125–141). Amsterdam: John Benjamins.

Vine, B., & Marra, M. (2017). The Wellington language in the workplace project: Creating stability through flexibility. In M. Marra & P. Warren (Eds.), *Linguist at work: Festschrift for Janet Holmes* (pp. 177–197). Wellington: Victoria University Press.

Vine, B., Marra, M., & Holmes, J. (2021). Male eldercare workers in New Zealand. To appear in J. McDowell (Ed), *De-gendering gendered occupations: Analysing communicative practices in the workplace* (pp. 17–40). Abingdon: Routledge.

Williams, H. W. (1971). *A dictionary of the Maori language.* Wellington: Government Printing Office.

Wolf, J., & Rosenberg, T. (2012). How individual scholars can reduce the rigor-relevance gap in management research. *Business Research, 5*, 178–196.

3

What Is Professional in a Professional Magazine? Using Corpus Analysis to Identify Specializedness in Professional Discourse and Culture

Fanny Domenec and Philippe Millot

Introduction

Over the last years, the analysis of professional discourse has focused on diverse linguistic and discursive data, ranging from written business genres and oral interactions among practitioners to the use of digital tools, in a variety of contexts like medicine, law or the corporate world, among others (Gunnarsson et al. 2014; Alessi and Jacobs 2016). Some studies have reflected on ethnographic approaches to professional discourses (Lønsmann 2016; Briguglio 2016), while others have focused on specific genres of professional discourse (Lazzeretti 2016; Alessi 2016) or

F. Domenec (✉)
Université Paris 2 Panthéon-Assas, Paris, France
e-mail: fanny.domenec@u-paris2.fr

P. Millot
Jean Moulin University Lyon 3, Lyon, France
e-mail: philippe.millot@univ-lyon3.fr

G. Jacobs, S. Decock (eds.), *Good Data in Business and Professional Discourse Research and Teaching*, Communicating in Professions and Organizations,
https://doi.org/10.1007/978-3-030-61757-8_3

on the construction of professional discourse and narratives (Mishler 2014; Hydén 2014; Hall et al. 2014). These analyses, which provide insightful contributions to the characterization of professional discourse and its uses, are based on an interdisciplinary approach:

> The field of business and professional discourse research is richly interdisciplinary, attracting scholars in applied linguistics and discourse studies as well as sociology, management, marketing and information systems. (Alessi and Jacobs 2016, p. 2)

However, it seems that so far rather little attention has been paid to the characterization of the specialized nature of professional domains. In this chapter, we aim to gain an insight into the "specializedness" of professional language and discourse, reflecting on the data and methods that can be used in the field of English for Specific Purposes (ESP). Indeed, as several researchers have showed (Benedetto 2017; Charret-Del Bove et al. 2017; Peynaud 2015; Mémet and Hillion 2004) and just like the various disciplines mentioned above, ESP provides relevant tools based on corpus analyses, to analyse specific data related to the professional milieu and its actors. Our work is based on Anthony Saber's (2016, p. 2) definition of specialized English as a variety of English "that can be observed in a given perimeter of society, delineated by professional or disciplinary boundaries". As such, we believe that specialized discourses should be seen as an insightful entry point into the professional world and can have "practical relevance" (Wolf and Rosenberg 2012, p. 178) for practitioners, by identifying a set of common needs and practices that constitute professional specialization.

Following Alessi and Jacobs (2016, p. 2), we take "["business" and "professional"] to refer to language and communication in or around the workplace". Yet, the very concept of "professional specializedness" raises several challenges as it applies not only to multiple domains and sectors of activity, but also to multiple professions. The professions chosen for this study—namely ethics and compliance officers and records and information managers—are cases in point in that both professions share some features in terms of language and communication: they are generally set in the corporate world, they both deal with compliance. However, as professions, they both display specific features simply because they fulfill different corporate functions and, therefore, call upon different conceptual worlds (ethics on the one hand, and information on the other).

The position of ethics and compliance officer, also known as "ethics officer" or "chief ethics and compliance officer", is described by Sampson as "a relatively new kind of function" (2016, p. 70). Following recent scandals in the business world (the Enron scandal in 2001, the 2008 crisis, the Volkswagen or the Wells Fargo cases in 2014 and 2016, respectively), companies now need professionals specifically trained in ethical and reputational issues. As such, ethics and compliance management differs from more traditional positions like the general counsel, the CSR team or the chief financial officer (Sampson 2016, p. 70). This "relatively new function" (Gnazzo 2011, p. 534) is often distinguished from compliance, which focuses on norms and regulations while ethics is described as more proactive: chief ethics and compliance officers are usually in charge of drafting and communicating the ethical values and culture that define the identity of the company. They also make sure that employees can voice their concerns and be listened to, respond to crises involving ethical issues and report directly to the CEO and C-suite.

The position of records and information manager is much older since managing corporate documents and archives has always been part of corporate life. However, since the 1980s and the development of information technology, the number of corporate documents has dramatically increased, especially with digital documents such as emails. As the magazines under study show, the increase has led to a renewal of the profession which is now confronted with IT issues such as Big Data, GDPR (General Data Protection Regulation) or data security risks.[1] Today, the domain involves professionals who, depending on their academic background and experience, deal with information and data management from organizational, technical, and legal perspectives. These managers work in various business contexts but it seems that most of them work in large-size organizations where information processing, especially since the "digital revolution", has become a critical aspect of management in general.

Just like academic journals which contribute to the making of disciplines, professional magazines play a major role in the construction and evolution of professions. As a genre set, they aim not only to transmit specialized knowledge to a given professional community, but they also help build the identity of the professional community, through the circulation and evolution of specialized language. Indeed, we follow the assumption that "the use of language and discourse in the professions shapes social reality, and reproduces and maintains social activities and relations" (Gunnarsson et al. 2014, p. 3). Although three studies have focused respectively on the digitalization of professional magazines (MacColl 1997), on their ranking among scientific publications (Peffers and Ya 2003) and on the role of editorial processes in the selection of news (Nijholt et al. 2014), it seems that professional magazines have not yet been considered as fully-fledged objects of study in the field of business and professional discourse research. However, these documents appear as reflecting authentic communicative practices, as they are issued by and targeted to restricted discourse communities (Swales 2016) of professionals in different fields. By choosing professional magazines as an entry point to characterize professional specializedness, we favor a "context-oriented", linguistic approach to genre sets (Jacobs 1999; Resche 2003; Gledhill and Kübler 2016), focused on "the analysis of language in its social or cultural context, as well as a focus on language forms as they occur in actual text (hence an overlap between the terms 'context' and 'co-text')" (Gledhill and Kübler 2016, p. 27).

We argue that the relevance of professional magazines as an entry point into specialization is twofold. First, professional magazines provide insight into a form of epistemological specializedness, as they display "specialized language in action" (Resche 2003, p. 38). Several studies have shown that specialized language and discourses can be used as a starting point to grasp the culture and domain-specific expectations of the professional milieu under study (Resche 2013, 2016; Van der Yeught 2017, 2018; Domenec and Resche 2018). Second, professional magazines are issued by and for professionals. As such, they are part of the "written [...] and digital communication in business and professional settings" (Alessi and Jacobs 2016, p. 1). Following Alessi and Jacobs (2016, p. 4) we argue that the study of professional magazines can be conceived as a "non-invasive access to practitioners' discursive contexts and practices", which makes them particularly relevant for the study of professional and business discourse. In their paper on the "rigor-relevance gap in management research", Wolf and Rosenberg (2012) insist on the need for "operational validity", [by focusing] on variables that practitioners can influence or design" (Wolf and Rosenberg 2012, p. 181). We argue that for each domain under study (ethics management and information and records management), professional magazines do "reflect internal aspects" (Wolf and Rosenberg 2012, p. 185) or "internal structures and processes" (Wolf and Rosenberg 2012, p. 187) experienced by practitioners on a daily basis. This practical approach appears, among others, in articles dealing with new regulations or systems that have a direct impact on professional norms or processes, or in the promotion of professional events like conferences, training programmes and certifications that shape the culture of the profession (Isani 2004).

In addition, we agree that "[m]anagement research is practically relevant as soon as it helps shift managers' understanding of their firms, the environment, and their jobs" (Belfiore and Bennet 2008, in Wolf and Rosenberg 2012, p. 181). From a functional perspective, we posit that whatever the specialized domain under study, professional magazines display common features that could be seen as prototypical of a more general professional specializedness. As such, the careful analysis of specializedness in professional magazines could help practitioners change their view on these tools, which could be seen as inherently part of their professional culture and practice.

This paper is organized as follows: we first define professional magazines and why they can be seen as authentic data to study professional practices and specializedness (see Section "Characterizing the Evolution of Professional Specialization through Language: A Bottom-up Approach to Investigate Professions"), then we focus on data collection and methodology. The results present four main aspects of professional specialization in professional magazines: the distribution of general semantic categories; domain-specific terms for each professional magazine; domain-bound collocational patterns, and the strategies used for conveying specialized information. As such, professional magazines are useful entry points to characterize emerging professional milieus. Not only do they help professionals in the field define the norms that regulate their field, but the data they contain can also be useful to students or other practitioners to get familiar with this field.

Theoretical Framework

Recent Evolutions in the Study of Professional Discourse: Accessing Reliable and Relevant Data

The study of professional discourse was born in the fields of sociology and ethnography of communication with the works of Gumperz (1982) on interactional sociolinguistics, conversational analysis (Sacks 1972) or microsociology (Goffman 1967). These approaches have generated datasets that highlight how discourse allows professionals to enact their social roles (e.g., doctor/patient, superior/subordinate) in specific contexts.

With the growing need for teaching languages in professional contexts and the advent of corpus linguistics in the late 1990s and early 2000s, the analytical focus on social roles gradually shifted towards the communicative functions of text types, leading to a focus on new kinds of datasets of professional discourse. Specialized corpora of professional genres have indeed been collected widely since Bhatia's seminal work on professional discourse (Bhatia 1993) and they have somewhat renewed our approach to what counts as data in professional discourse. The first renewal lies in the identification of a direct relationship between the communicative purpose of a text and its lexico-grammatical features. The second renewal lies in a refinement of the context which, as many specialized corpora illustrate, now embraces myriads of parameters. A third renewal lies in pointing to an "enriched" version of professional discourse with technologies enabling researchers to add visualizing tools, images or videos, paving the way to ever thicker descriptions of professional discourse.

Nowadays, professional genres remain an essential tool for the study of professional discourses. In her seminal article, Carolyn Miller (1984, p. 160) defined genres as "typified rhetorical actions based in recurrent situations" and concluded that:

> For the critic, genres can serve both as an index to cultural patterns and as tools for exploring the achievements of particular speakers and writers; for the student, genres serve as keys to understanding how to participate in the actions of a community (Miller 1984, p. 165)

Although we do agree with the implications for critics and students, our approach to sampling is different: we put communicative purposes in the background, to focus on the concept of "professional domain", which we consider as a specific branch in the theory of specialized domains (another type of specializedness could be disciplines, for instance, see Percebois 2006; Petit 2010; Van der Yeught 2018). As Millot (2019) suggests, this "professional specializedness" should be evidence-based and would be threefold: theoretical (through concepts that are specific to a domain and which can mostly be found in research articles), mediated (the transmission of theoretical knowledge via publications by professional associations) and practical (the discourses that implement concrete actions in the domain, *i.e.*, job ads, informal expert discourse, ISO norms or patents). In this framework, a complete "professional discourse" corpus gathers texts (analog or digital) taken from the three different categories mentioned above (theory, mediation, practice). In this specific chapter, we focus on the "mediation" category, using the example of professional magazines.

Defining Professional Magazines

Nijholt et al. (2014, p. 2) define professional magazines as "[...] practitioner-oriented magazines [that] aim to inform targeted professional groups on managerial topics and form a recognizable category of publications in the field of business media". Generally published on a monthly basis, professional magazines are "often glossy, full-color publications [that] are seen as representing distinct 'speech communities' since they are often geared to audiences with specific professional interests and can be affiliated to professional associations [...]" (Nijholt et al. 2014, p. 4). Indeed, *Information Management* (IM) and *Compliance and Ethics Professional* (CEP), the two professional magazines selected for this chapter, are issued by an association for records management (formerly known as the Association of Record Managers and Administrators or ARMA) and the Society for Corporate Compliance and Ethics (SCCE), respectively.

In order to define professional magazines, it is important to understand that they do not constitute a genre *per se*. Indeed, if we follow Miller's definition (1984, p. 153), "[...] a rhetorically sound definition of genre must be centered not on the substance or the form of discourse but on the action it is used to accomplish". One of the characteristics of professional magazines is that their varied content aims to accomplish several "rhetorical actions" (ibid.): information and/or popularization, promotion of the domain through various pieces of writing, storytelling or advertising for books or collective events, advice to newcomers in the field, etc. As such, professional magazines should therefore be regarded as a "genre set", comprising several genres, some of which have been characterized in previous studies such as editorials, professional stories or print ads.

Although they do not form one single genre, it is true that professional magazines share some features of "occluded genres" (Swales 1996), issued by specialists for specialists: first, they are addressed to distinct groups or individuals and written by professionals, not by scholars. As such, professional magazines are "not themselves part of the research record", yet they are "seriously invested with demonstrated scholarship and seriously concerned with representing their authors in a favorable light". In addition, they also contain information that can be "useful to newcomers and that may not be learnt in the academic literature" (Swales 1996, pp. 47–48).

Defining a Profession

Although the term "profession" is widely used on a daily basis, it seems essential to define the concept at this stage: following Wolf and Rosenberg (2012, p. 190), "we believe that clear definitions are especially crucial for achieving practical relevance". For practitioners in an emerging and/or evolving professional field, the very definition of what a profession is can raise questions related to legitimacy or relevance. Indeed, characterizing professions has frequently been described as problematic (Cogan 1955; Torstendahl 2005; Saks 2012; Buhai 2012). Some researchers have underscored the importance of context (Adams 2010), while others have focused on the importance of functional and symbolic aspects:

> Professions have attained a strategic position in modern industrial society as the occupational groups whose task it is to develop and apply abstract and technical knowledge to important problems of everyday life. The task, which is essential to the smooth running of the industrialized business economy and which must be carried on by highly trained personnel, is institutionalized in the various professional roles. (Huntington 1956, p. 87)

Because membership is a prerequisite to have access to the professional magazines, we believe that they provide insight into the communicative needs of the two professional discourse communities (information management and ethics and compliance) who share "a broadly agreed set of goals" (Swales 2016, p. 2). These goals are described in the mission statements of the two associations that issue the professional magazines under study. The mission statement of ARMA International states that the association aims to "empower the community of information professionals to advance their careers, organizations, and the profession.[2]" Similarly, the SCCE "exists to champion ethical practice and compliance standards and to provide the necessary resources for ethics and compliance professionals and others who share these principles.[3]"

These collective visions could be identified with a form of "specialized collective intentionality", recently described by Van der Yeught (2016, 2017, 2018) as the foundation of specialized domains. Van der Yeught (2018, p. 3) advocates an "[…] intentional approach to specialized languages [that] does not start from an analysis of language, but from the study of the mental states that generate language". It seems to us that this theory is particularly relevant to study the "ins" of professional discourse, in other words, to understand how the creation and evolution of the specialized language in the professional magazines goes together with changes in the professional discourse and milieu. Following Searle's theory of intentionality, Van der Yeught assumes that:

> […] "to specialise" may be defined as one such type of intentional state where the mind is consistently directed towards one and the same object, in a focused, selective, repetitive and durable way and under a particular aspectual shape (Van der Yeught 2016, p. 47). For example, someone "specialising" in water perceived as H_2O is perhaps developing a chemist's

> interest in water that may materialise into some form of speciality like chemistry. Similarly, the various aspectual shapes of the sun […] may give rise to various forms of specialisation although the object is the same: astronomy, the study of religions or solar technology. (Van der Yeught 2018, p. 12).

In the case of professional associations, the object (information management or corporate ethics and compliance) is considered as requiring a specific training, skills and know-how, to apply knowledge to a specific field, rather than a mere legal constraint or philosophical concept. Following Van der Yeught's theory of specialized domains, it is the combination of several individual behaviors and attitudes to a specific object that gives rise to a specialized domain:

> At a higher level of organisation, […], individuals may establish or join associations with professional and/or disciplinary objectives which form fully fledged specialised communities. In doing so they generally immerse themselves in a body of knowledge and know-how harnessed to serve a common purpose—a specialised domain or speciality—which results from the accumulated experience of people sharing the same intentionalities. (Van der Yeught 2018, p. 16)

Specialized domains can only exist and work through the creation of social facts and norms, as "[…] all specialised institutions create an infinite amount of institutional facts to serve their intentional purposes" (Van der Yeught 2018, p. 19). In order to define and implement this "social reality", specialized languages are created to convey the norms and principles of a given specialized domain. In the case of professional associations in general, institutional facts are created via the process of "structuration" (Greenwood et al. 2002, p. 59), described as "a process of gradual maturity and specification of roles, behaviors and interactions of organizational communities" (ibid.). As such, professional associations play a major role in defining the profession, but also the norms and rules that govern it:

> Specifically, associations enable the construction of accounts delineating the domain of a profession—that is, the portfolios of activities and services

> over which members claim jurisdictional exclusivity—and of accounts specifying conditions of membership: that is, who can practice authoritatively within that jurisdiction, and how. (Greenwood et al. 2002, pp. 59–60).

Several studies have shown that a profession is not a stable object and can undergo phases of "deinstitutionalization" and "reinstitutionalization" (Greenwood et al. 2002, p. 59). Professional magazines are one of the tools used by professional associations to share information on new actors, ideas or regulations that may redefine the scope of a profession.

Characterizing the Evolution of Professional Specialization through Language: A Bottom-Up Approach to Investigate Professions

To gain insight into the specific meaning of specialized languages, appropriate tools like glossaries, dictionaries and descriptions should be investigated, in order to master specialized languages and natural second languages alike (Van der Yeught 2018). Although specialized magazines are different from glossaries or encyclopedia, we argue that they can be used to study "the expression of specializedness in language" (Van der Yeught 2018, p. 4). Indeed, to Nijholt et al. (2014, p. 3), professional magazines are usually seen as "an empirical means to study the evolving popularity of particular ideas", but also as "disseminators of management ideas". The language and discourse found in professional magazines thus derive from a specialized community, built around specific rules and norms: "[…] specialised collective intentionality generates specialized languages [SLs] thanks to constitutive rules that create social reality" (Van der Yeught 2018, p. 4). Professional magazines are part of the category of business media, which "[…] form an important "strategic checkpoint" for producers of management ideas, since they perform a gatekeeping role […] which may block or facilitate the further dissemination of ideas […]" (Nijholt et al. 2014, p. 2).

> [...] the business media can 'draw widespread attention to progressive management rhetorics championing particular management techniques' (Abrahamson 1996, p. 269), but also [...] influence corporate agendas (Carroll 2010) and [...] define, frame and (de) legitimate events and corporate activities (Grafström and Windell 2011; Hellgren et al. 2002; Vaara et al. 2006; Vergne 2011; Zavyalova et al. 2012) (Nijholt et al. 2014, p. 2)

As such, the language found in professional magazines participates in building the identity of the profession, via the definition and popularization of the rules and norms that are specific to each domain.

Methodology

Building Parallel Corpora in Specialized Professional Discourse

In order to characterize the specializedness of professional magazines, we evaluate how specific the targeted domains are regarding general language and how specific they are regarding each other. Our corpus-driven study is based on parallel corpora that seek to represent two different professional domains as they appear through magazines published by professional societies (see Table 3.1). Professional magazines, therefore, form the data used for analysing "specializedness".

As such, our corpus provides a powerful entry point to two specialized cultures. The magazines indeed comprise text types (e.g., editorials, news reports, in-depth articles) that shed light on various aspects of these cultures such as new trends and tools, case studies, core professional concepts, or shared values and missions. They also provide information about the two professional communities they represent. First, the articles (in-depth articles in particular) are written by expert professionals who not only share their expertise but also provide information about their own profiles (e.g. the companies they work for, their degrees and certifications). Secondly, the magazines present or at least mention business contexts (companies or business sectors) that can help locate the domains on the business map.

Table 3.1 Parallel corpora of professional magazines: *Compliance and Ethics Professional* and *Information Management*

	Main subject areas	Period	Issues (n)	Size (in number of words)
Compliance and Ethics Professional	Business ethics, compliance, corporate culture, risk management, accountability	2013–2016	24	800,000
Information Management	Records and information management, knowledge management, corporate archiving, digital technology	2013–2016	24	540,000

However, it is important to mention that magazines do not entirely represent business realities in these domains. Rather, magazines are a particular discourse type which undeniably conveys a promotional, positive "picture" of the specialized communities in question. For example, we have realised many professional magazine articles were often shared on the professional network LinkedIn by the authors themselves who clearly use their own texts as strategies for presenting themselves as experts within their professional communities. The promotional dimension of professional magazines also regularly appears through passages that clearly "sell the domain" to other professionals, as the extract below illustrates.

> I was able to share general RIM [records and information management] knowledge and methodologies so they had a better understanding of how things worked and what we could do for them. (*Information Manager*, July-August 2014, p. 44)

Retrieving Specializedness from the Corpora

Specializedness is a complex phenomenon which emerges through all parts of language and which may be realized at various text levels, from word- or token level, to longer stretches including phraseology and even genres (Gledhill and Kübler 2016). In this exploratory study of professional magazines, we essentially focus on short units of meaning to identify what constitutes the specializedness of compliance and ethics, on the one hand, and that of records and information management, on the other. The reason for our choice of short units lies in the fact that the token level and the phraseological level provide valuable entry points—though not the only ones—into terms which form the basis of how specialized a text is.

The specializedness of our data was retrieved through various corpus-driven strategies. The first strategy consisted in examining to what extent existing semantic categories could yield specialized data from our corpus. This part of the study was conducted by using the WMatrix software (Rayson 2008) which enabled us to apply broad semantic tags to both corpora. Semantic tag frequency patterns for each tag were then compared in order to see whether some areas of meaning were more salient in one domain than in the other. This approach enabled us to retrieve some specialized data from the corpus but its potential proved limited when it came to identifying how specific one corpus was compared to the other.

To analyse the specificity[4] of either corpus, we therefore conducted a keyness analysis by using the other corpus as "reference". As Wierzbicka (1997, p. 156) claims, keywords are first and foremost a cultural concept in that they represent a "focal point around which entire cultural domains are organized". However, as Scott and Tribble (2006, p. 65) also remind us, keywords are a "textual matter" which, in our corpus-driven approach, may be defined as "words which are significantly more frequent in a sample of text than would be expected, given their frequency in a large general reference corpus" (Stubbs 2010, p. 25).

In this part of our study, we hypothesise that the chances of obtaining the specific data from each corpus are much higher when the contexts and the genres are similar. Indeed, comparing specialised corpora with "general English" ones would only yield data that is "not general", thus leaving behind some data that are not necessarily relevant for the characterization of specialised domains and discourses. However, using the other corpus as a "mirror" enables us to focus on the culture-specific or specialized data that constitute each corpus.

Table 3.2 Target corpora and reference corpora for keyword analysis

Target corpus	Target corpus size	Reference corpus	Reference corpus size
Information Management (all issues)	540,000	Compliance and Ethics Professional (all issues)	800,000
Compliance and Ethics Professional (latest issues)	330,000	Information Management (all issues)	540,000

A technical problem that corpus linguists face when they conduct keyness analyses is to make sure that the target corpus (the corpus we seek to analyse) is smaller than the reference corpus (the corpus used as "reference" in the comparison). Since the CEP corpus was larger than the IM corpus, we created a 330,000-word sample of the CEP corpus (see Table 3.2) by focusing on the latest issues of Compliance and Ethics Professional so that the CEP corpus sample could efficiently be compared with a larger, reference corpus.

Identifying Degrees of Specialization through Collocational Profiles

What makes corpora "specialised" is not merely the fact that they originate from specialised contexts. Specializedness, as Gledhill (2011) suggests, is based on the idea that the main terms in a domain tend to generate special collocational profiles which could potentially make them markers of specializedness. In order to test our hypothesis, we created a procedure which enabled us to systematically compare collocational profiles across contexts. First, we retrieved a collocate list for the three most frequent terms in each domain ("compliance", "ethics" and "company" for Compliance and Ethics, and "information", "management", and "records" for Information Management). Collocate lists were then compared with one another in order to see to what extent the two professional domains shared the same items. Finally, we conducted a second comparison with general usage in order to see to what extent degrees of specializedness could be identified from one professional domain to another, and from professional domains to general usage.

"Inter-professional" comparisons were conducted by using the Antconc collocational tool which enabled us to retrieve collocate lists from which the 50 most frequent lexical items were selected. The size of the collocational span was voluntarily broad (4L, 4R) since we were focusing on semantic prosodies and not the identification of typical expressions. "Professional-general" comparisons were conducted by using the Corpus of Contemporary American English (COCA) which enabled us to retrieve collocate lists for the six terms with the same span (4L, 4R).

Identifying Mediation Features

We conducted a preliminary study of "mediation features" by looking at how professional information was conveyed to the readers who may not be experts in each and every subject. The first method consisted in retrieving words and phrases that helped authors make complex notions accessible to readers (e.g., "the term…", "the concept…", "defined as", "known as", etc.). The second method consisted in examining cognitive metaphors helping readers understand complex business situations and processes. Metaphorical expressions were retrieved by looking at incongruous semantic categories ("the world and the environment", "entertainment, sports and games") in WMatrix and, as a complementary approach, by manually analyzing a sample of twenty in-depth magazine articles (ten from the latest issues) in which metaphors were likely to be found because the subjects were rather new or complex—and therefore required images that paraphrased the specialized meaning.

Results

Distribution of Semantic Categories

Figure 3.1 presents a bird's eye view of the semantic configuration of each corpus. First, our results show that both magazines cover the entire spectrum of semantic categories as they are defined by WMatrix. Secondly, it appears that both domains share a very similar semantic configuration:

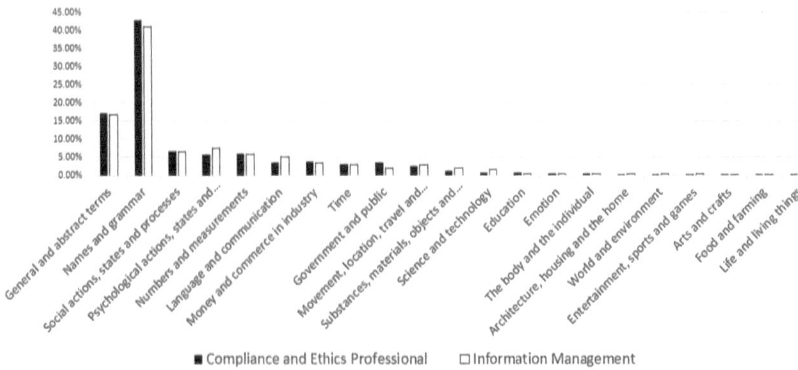

Fig. 3.1 Proportions of semantic tags in two professional magazines: *Compliance and Ethics Professional* compared with *Information Management*

the categories emerge in more or less similar proportions in both corpora, with "general abstract terms" and "names and grammar" representing the most frequent categories, followed by other, less frequent ones such as social actions, psychological actions, numbers and measurements, etc. This finding suggests that, in a way, professional varieties are not separate entities from "general English" as they cover the entire spectrum of meanings, which confirms the already mentioned continuum between general and specialized languages (Resche 1999). First, this semantic variety can be explained by the fact that each domain is used in many kinds of professional situations. Information management and compliance and ethics are used in all kinds of corporate or industrial sectors, which tends to generate meanings that differ from the "core concepts" of the domain. Secondly, the semantic variety may also be explained by the fact that each professional domain mobilizes metaphors that bring counterintuitive semantic categories to the surface. For example, the famous (and very frequent) "cloud" metaphor largely contributes to the salience of the "world and environment" category in information management. Additional examples of metaphors are provided further in this section.

Quite paradoxically in a way, general semantic categories can help us retrieve specialized data from the corpus. For example, a closer look at the "social actions, states and processes" reveals that the most important semantic field in both domains by far is the "power relationship" which

Word	Semtag	Frequency	Relative Frequency
management	S7.1+	1323	0.40
managing	S7.1+	249	0.07
control	S7.1+	183	0.05
manage	S7.1+	181	0.05
manager	S7.1+	147	0.04
managers	S7.1+	146	0.04
director	S7.1+	104	0.03
executive	S7.1+	104	0.03
Chief	S7.1+	101	0.03
accountability	S7.1+	101	0.03

Fig. 3.2 The most frequent words from the "power relationships" semantic sub-category in Wmatrix (screen capture from the IM corpus)

includes words that are naturally frequent in business contexts such as "management", "executive" or "accountability" (see Fig. 3.2).

Therefore, it seems that these semantic categories, albeit belonging to the "general English" paradigm, can help us identify specialized data from the corpus. However, these categories are also misleading because domain-bound terminology, which constitutes a great deal of linguistic body of professional magazines, tends to escape general English categories in such a way that many terms may pass entirely unnoticed. For example, terms such as "compliance" or "records" have specific meanings in their specialized domains which makes them hardly identifiable when one adopts a corpus-driven approach based on a general English framework. In other words, and as the next sections seek to show, identifying what counts as data in professional discourse from a corpus perspective requires considering not only data from general semantic frameworks but also from others which will help us retrieve the professional substance from the corpus.

Domain-specific Terms

As explained earlier, domain-specific terms were identified by conducting a keyword analysis based on using the two corpora as "reference" corpora for each other. As hypothesised, our method yielded a list of terms which

Table 3.3 Keywords in Information Management (CEP corpus as reference)

Item	Log likelihood	Log ratio
Records	4082.64	4.95
Information	3268.54	2.51
Data	2372.9	2.42
Rim[a]	1577.27	8.98
Retention	1274.09	4.96
IG	1108.04	5.01
Cloud	1059.3	4.4
ARMA	826.43	10.6
Electronic	793.07	3.62
CRM	750.45	4.97
Security	727.78	2.34
E-mail	694.31	7.43
Principles	672.73	2.81
Storage	664.31	5.52
E-discovery	645.16	6.77
Privacy	642.85	2.24
Digital	509.13	3.87
FAI	494.94	9.86
Management	473.89	1.26
Preservation	464.83	6.88
Stored	452.95	5.77
Recordkeeping	450.9	7.79
Software	440.19	3.45
Organizations	431.97	1.42
Technology	421.57	2.53
Disposition	398.15	8.59
Discovery	395.21	4.14
Contacted	387.6	5.43
Big	361.3	2.49
Users	359.01	3.03
Access	331.43	2.21
File	316.55	3.51
Mobile	315.93	3.96
Governance	306.3	1.69

[a]Records and Information Management

define the domains of information management on the one hand (see Table 3.3) and compliance and ethics on the other (see Table 3.4).

Table 3.3 shows that the specificity of the IM corpus is based on a conceptual universe that describes the domain from different categories. The first category may be termed the "core-concepts" which are a set of fundamental terms (e.g., "records", "information", "data", "RIM",

Table 3.4 Keywords in CEP sample (IM corpus as reference)

Item	Log likelihood	Log ratio
Compliance	6150.23	3.66
Ethics	4442.26	7.55
You	1080.95	1.83
SCCE	829.73	9.98
I	818.04	2.2
Ethical	710.34	5.48
Your	686.48	1.53
We	618.4	1.84
Company	556.85	1.92
My	504.73	3.72
Corporate	480.64	2.11
CCEP	441.1	9.07
Our	427.3	1.87
Culture	350.54	2.77
Me	312.26	5.01
Us	292.35	2.38
Training	291.44	1.85
Officer	290.71	2.64
Compliance professionals	287.99	7.51
Corruption	280.39	5.59
Board	250.21	2.67
Do	245.84	1.04
Misconduct	242	5.11
Feature	241.17	3.32
Scces	238.04	8.18
CCEP-I	237.28	8.17
Program	236.17	1.03
Conduct	231.83	2.49
Investigations	220.7	3.18
Fcpa	207.62	7.98
Employees	204.88	1.09
Values	199.6	3.65
Anti-corruption	186.33	7.82
Officers	183.07	2.78
Academies	180.24	7.78
Bribery	179.38	6.85

"retention"). Unsurprisingly, as shown in Table 3.3, the core concepts for CEP revolve around "ethics" and "compliance". "Company", "corporate", "employees" and "board" suggest that the core concepts are to be implemented throughout the company as a whole, via a specific professional "culture" and "values". The second category corresponds to the ongoing issues and concerns in the field of information management: "privacy", "Big" data, or "mobile" technology are subjects that are recurrently discussed in the magazine. In the field of ethics and compliance, legal issues and regulation are core issues: "(anti)-corruption", "bribery" and "misconduct" are frequently discussed in CEP, just like the FCPA (Foreign Corrupt Practices Act) and "investigations" conducted by regulators. The third category is an institutional one: in IM, IG (Information Governance) refers to the organisation of information at corporate level, while acronyms such as FAI (First Article Inspection) and CRM (Certified Records Manager) refer to professional certifications. The need for certification has also become a key issue in the compliance and ethics profession, with frequent references to "training", "program" and "academy" in CEP, and more specifically to the "CCEP" (Certified Compliance and Ethics Professional) and "CCEP-1" exams, which reflect an emerging professionalization of the field with "officer(s)" and "compliance professionals". The fourth category contains the more general words showing a strong, technological orientation of the domain of information management, at least when compared with compliance and ethics. The frequent use of personal pronouns ("you", "I", "your", "we", "my", "our", "me" and "us") in CEP underscores the almost systematic use of storytelling in the articles, putting forward the personal experience of contributors, as well as their own expertise in the field.

Domain-bound Collocational Patterns

Our study shows that collocational profiles of the most frequent terms are domain-specific. Although CEP and IM share some terms such as "company", "compliance", "information" or "ethics", those terms are associated with different collocates. Since the two domains are studied from the same genre set, we hypothesise that the collocational profile of these terms is specialized in that each term tends to mobilize word associations that describe the domain.

Figures 3.3 and 3.4 seek to illustrate what may be termed "specialised collocational profiles". For example, the word "company", although it is used in both domains, is associated with a certain number of collocates in the CEP corpus which are shared only to a limited extent in the IM corpus—the shared collocates refer to the general corporate context with words such as "business", "compliance", "employee", "financial" or "legal". In the CEP corpus, "company" collocates with words describing typical ethically sensitive contexts—words like "shell", "insurance", "pharmaceutical" were found to be frequent collocates—as well as words describing the world of ethics (e.g., "values", "leniency"). Shared collocates with general English usage—here represented by the COCA

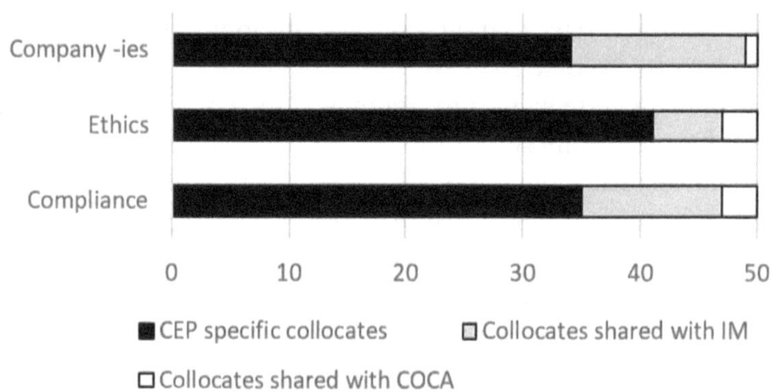

Fig. 3.3 Collocational profiles of the three most frequent terms in Compliance and Ethics: Proportion of shared collocates in the IM corpus and the COCA

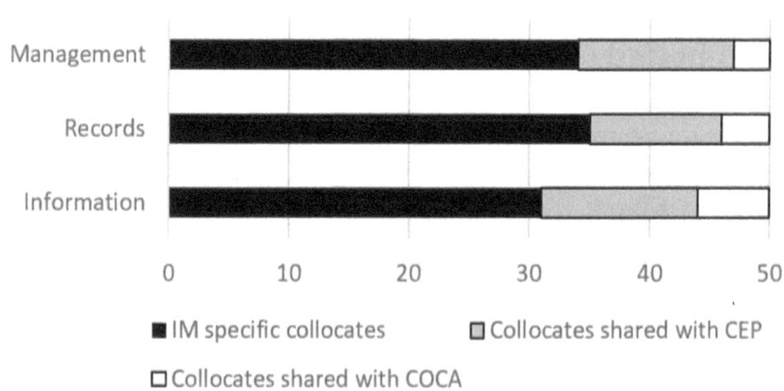

Fig. 3.4 Collocational profiles of the three most frequent terms in Information Management: Proportion of shared collocates in the CEP corpus and the COCA

corpus—decrease dramatically to a single case ("employee"). It is therefore reasonable to assume that the notion of company in the CEP domain is literally shaped by intentions of compliance and ethics professionals. As Figs. 3.3 and 3.4 show, a similar pattern can be observed with other frequent terms from the corpus.

This finding suggests that "specializedness" in professional discourse as represented through the two professional magazines under study, is not only characterized by the salience of particular terms or concepts but is also characterized by the specific contexts and practices, or cultures, in which those terms are used. The data found in IM and CEP thus displays a twofold specialization: first, a professional specialization, as opposed to general English (IM and CEP vs COCA), second, a professional and disciplinary specialization, depending on the business context (IM vs CEP). These different degrees of specialization show the necessity of diversifying data.

Mediation Discourse Features

Specialized features are a major characteristic of professional magazines but the mediation of specialist information in professional magazines reaches beyond the mere presentation of technical facts. Rather, "specializedness" in this particular genre set includes strategies that make this information accessible to readers who, although they may be experts, may not be entirely comfortable with particular subjects. In this section, we explore two strategies that we found were particularly salient: the use of formulaic sequences which introduce explanatory content and the use of metaphors which are used as strategies for clarifying complex meanings.

Formulaic Sequences Introducing Explanatory Content

Formulaic sequences (e.g., TERM + "is defined", "for example" + CLAUSE, "the term" + CLAUSE, TERM + means that, etc.) are probably the simplest forms of expression that help readers understand specialist information in that they introduce definitions, illustrations and content that seeks to clarify what may be considered obscure by readers

Table 3.5 Cases of metalanguage used for popularizing specialized discourse

Phrases	CEP	IM	Total
V+ defined, a definition of	295	381	676
For example	204	268	472
Mean* that	49	315	364
Refer* to	78	73	151
Shows (that)	81	58	139
The concept	80	21	101
Subj. + involves	64	26	90
For instance	46	40	86
Known as	20	14	34
The word	26	7	33
The term	11	16	27
The phrase	23	1	24
Subj. implies	11	8	19
Total	988	1230	2218

*Stem

even though some of them might be specialists in the field. As Table 3.5 shows, those sequences were regularly found in both corpora.

The sentences below present typical cases of such sequences where specialist information (underlined) is framed by "metalanguage" (highlighted in bold):

- For the purpose of this article, *the cloud* **refers to** any service provider that offers technology or tools that are directly accessible from the internet. (IM)
- Forrester **has defined** *big data* **as** "the practices and technology that close the gap between the data available and the ability to turn that data into business insight." (IM)
- *Ethics*, broadly speaking, **involves identifying rights and wrongs**. (CEP)
- **A broadly used term** "*self-regulatory organizations*" (SROs) encompass **various types of entities** that seek to regulate their members' and others' activities (CEP)
- The **term originates from the concept of** affixing stamps on a document to demonstrate the tax was paid (IM)

- **The phrase** *"anything of value,"* **although undefined, has been interpreted to** include excessive meals, gifts, discounts, entertainment, and travel expenses, as well as the promise of future employment. (CEP)

Metaphors and Thought Experiments

Apart from formulaic sequences, we found a great deal of metaphorical discourse with cognitive metaphors that are typical of the professional world (BUSINESS IS A ROAD, BUSINESS IS A GAME). This kind of discourse regularly occurs with domain-bound concepts, typically along short spans of text, as the examples below seek to illustrate (the specialized concepts are underlined and metaphorical discourse is highlighted in bold).

- A *career* in compliance: A not so **straight and narrow path** (CEP)
- *RIM* **has crossed path with** privacy for decades (IM).
- It often takes **a winding road to** end up a compliance officer. (CEP)

Metaphorical discourse may also develop into longer stretches of text, where metaphors are used to "describe new phenomena or logical connections" (Hoffman 1985, pp. 332–333)

- Just like **quarterbacks**, *RIM professionals* have a number of responsibilities once the "**game**" or project, has begun. (IM)
- Employees can be asked to follow the rules of the *information governance* **road**, just as they must follow the **traffic rules of the road**, provided the rules are **practicable.** (IM)

In professional magazines, metaphors can also have an argumentative function: some are used to establish the legitimacy of the profession, and convince the reader of the "soundness of a measure" (Domenec and Resche 2018, p. xii):

- In short, the *IGMM* helps put the work into perspective as being part of a whole—not just random little pieces, but **tiles that are part of an intentional mosaic.** (IM)

- […] the *IGMM* are **signposts that point out current position, future direction**, and the means for getting the program—and yourself—from one place to the next. (IM)
- Because [the responsibilities of Compliance] should encompass independent review and assessment of **the second line-of-defense** Risk Management function, [compliance] should be separately categorized as **a third line of defense** within the organization's ERM framework, with Internal Audit as the fourth line. (CEP)
- In dealing with the client noted above I concluded that they had bought into the "*compliance*" model. They were **"hooked" on the opiates** of *compliance and best practices*. They saw no merit in *the "ethics" model*. After all, the law did not require more of them than they were already doing. Sadly, they were **three quarters of the way there**. They had successfully met the first three of the four elements needed to **avoid becoming a headline. To borrow a baseball metaphor**, they had **reached third base**. Their ethics and compliance program was a model of "best practices". But **you get no points for stranding a runner on third. Hitting a triple** may look great in your individual statistics, but **it doesn't count for much if the team loses** because you **failed to get the runner home**. They seemed willing to accept that **crossing the t's and dotting the i's** of compliance was their goal. (CEP)

Apart from metaphors, specialised information is also regularly made accessible through the presentation of "thought experiments". These experiments may be defined as imaginary scenarios which simulate prototypical professional situations helping readers project these situations to their own contexts.

- **Imagine** 1000 records center containers soaked by sewage water. (IM)
- But **imagine** that after several months, when hundreds or thousands of documents have been added to that single hanging folder, that specific document needs to be retrieved. (IM)
- Analogous to the person who engages in ethical decision making, we can **imagine** someone who builds an additional story to an existing structure without understanding the capacities of the building's foundation. (CEP6)

Conclusion

Low Specializedness and High Specializedness in Professional Magazines

Our results show that what counts as data in business discourse in professional magazines can be defined as a set of features conveying specialized or domain-bound knowledge to the members of the targeted professional community. Although specializedness is often seen as a matter of "technical jargon", our data show that specializedness is a multi-faceted phenomenon affecting many parts of discourse. These parts include meanings and collocational patterns that are specific to professional domains. They also include mediation discourse strategies which facilitate the transmission of expert knowledge as evidenced through the cases of formulaic sequences that introduce explanatory content, "business metaphors" as well as thought experiments that help professionals project themselves into situations and anticipate potential risks.

Specializedness in professional discourse emerged not as a discrete concept but, rather, as a continuum ranging from the sharing of common forms and meanings to highly specific features whose specificity can only be identified or interpreted by those who experience the culture of the specialized domains. "Low specializedness" may be characterized as the data shared by the two professional domains, which, as our study shows, consists of meanings describing the organizational part of professional power relationships and business cognitive metaphors such as "BUSINESS IS A ROAD, BUSINESS IS A GAME". "High specializedness", on the other hand, may be described as the words and collocational profiles that are entirely or mostly specific to a domain. Between high specializedness and low specializedness lies a grey area containing words and collocational profiles that are partly shared by the two domains and which will require further explorations.

Practical Implications

In this chapter, we have sought to propose a novel approach to the characterization of emerging professions, which could be useful to researchers and professionals who specialize in emerging or rapidly changing professions to various extents: being published by professional associations, professional magazines display "practical relevance", (Wolf and Rosenberg 2012, p. 181) and focus on "topics and phenomena with which practitioners in the field are actually confronted" (ibid.). In addition, their practical orientation makes them particularly relevant to focus on "variables that professionals can influence or design" (Wolf and Rosenberg 2012, p. 185). A regular overview of the data contained in professional magazines based on the four levels of analysis (semantic categories, terms, collocational patterns, mediation strategies) may be used to gain insight into specific "professional logics" (Demont 2013, p. 9), based on "specific ways of acting, specific discourses and specific professional situations" (ibid.). As such, the methodology proposed in this chapter may help quickly identify current challenges or problems in the profession under study, meeting the "timeliness" criterion (Wolf and Rosenberg 2012, p. 181).

For researchers, this methodology could be extended to other professions and domains, in order to further characterize the notion of professional specializedness. Because professional magazines provide readers with insights into professional spheres, both field specialists and ESP practitioners may benefit from their content. Professional magazines indeed provide readers with authentic material including news, case studies and in-depth analyses which may be used as ways of acquiring field knowledge and related language. Some articles could be studied in class in order to help students define some key concepts and their emergence and evolution and understand their practical implications. Some articles could also serve as a basis for case studies or role plays where the students would be confronted to actual challenges and decision-making processes. Professional magazines could also be used as a resource in the field of specialized translation.

Limits and Suggestions for Further Research

This chapter represents a first general approach to the characterization of professional specialization in professional magazines and we are well aware of the fact that each of the categories studied could be further developed. Other categories could also be analysed, like grammatical aspects or more in-depth analysis of syntactic features. In addition, the two professions under study (information management and corporate ethics) may be seen as close, as they both involve highly-qualified professionals and issues related to data and information. Hence, other professions could be studied, in order to generalize our findings and gain more insight into the general characteristics of professional discourse from a corpus-driven perspective. Finally, this chapter is part of a more general research project on professional discourses and should be seen as a step within a more general endeavour: professional magazines are one of the genre sets that are used in a professional domain in order to communicate information to professionals (mediation). However, a complete characterization of a professional domain should also take into account the theory of the domain (mainly though the analysis of research articles) and practices in the field (via onsite surveys, interviews and other ethnographic studies). By linking data collection and analysis to the context of production and circulation of professional knowledge, we advocate a global view on professional specialization, which could be replicated in a variety of domains.

Notes

1. For more information on each profession, see Section "Building Parallel Corpora in Specialized Professional Discourse".
2. https://www.arma.org/page/MissionAndVision, accessed 08/15/2019
3. https://www.corporatecompliance.org/about-society-corporate-compliance-and-ethics, accessed 08/15/2019
4. In this chapter, **specificity** is a rather technical notion which focuses on the differences between corpora. For example, when it comes to identifying specific lexicon, specificity overlaps with keyness. **Specializedness**, on the other hand, is considered as the general phenomenon which includes all sorts of cultural, discursive and linguistic data.

References

Abrahamson, E. (1996). Management fashion. *Academy of Management Review, 21*(1), 254–285.

Adams, T. L. (2010). Profession: a useful concept for sociological analysis?. *Canadian Review of Sociology/Revue canadienne de sociologie, 47*(1), 49–70.

Alessi, G. (2016). Standardizing the language of corporate internal investigative reports: Linguistic perspectives on professional writing practices. In G. Aless & G. Jacobs (Eds.), *The ins and outs of business and professional discourse research* (pp. 225–245). London: Palgrave Macmillan.

Alessi, G., & Jacobs, G. (2016). *The ins and outs of business and professional discourse research: Reflections on interacting with the workplace.* New York: Springer.

Benedetto, C. (2017). Les milieux professionnels et leur régulation: diversité terminologique et complexité organisationnelle. *ASp, 71*, 7–24.

Bhatia, V. (1993). *Analysing genre: Language use in professional setting.* London and New York: Routledge.

Briguglio, C. (2016). Gathering linguistic data from multinational companies: Inter-cultural communication in the workplace. In G. Alessi & G. Jacobs (Eds.), *The ins and outs of business and professional discourse research* (pp. 81–101). London: Palgrave Macmillan.

Buhai, S. L. (2012). Profession: A definition. *Fordham Urban Law Journal, 40*, 241.

Carroll, C. (2010). Should firms circumvent or work through the news media? *Public Relations Review, 36*, 278–280.

Charret-Del Bove, M., Millot, P., & Wozniak, S. (2017). Éditorial: Anglais de spécialité et milieux professionnels. *ASp. la revue du GERAS*, (71), 2–5.

Cogan, M. L. (1955). The problem of defining a profession. *The Annals of the American Academy of Political and Social Science, 297*, 105–111.

Demont, G. (2013). L'éthique professionnelle peut-elle se penser au singulier ? Le cas des formations dans le secteur de l'aide à la personne dépendante. *Recherche et pratiques pédagogiques en langues de spécialité.* https://doi.org/10.4000/apliut.3773.

Domenec, F., & Resche, C. (Eds.). (2018). *La Fonction argumentative de la métaphore dans les discours spécialisés.* Berne: Peter Lang.

Gledhill, C. (2011). The 'lexicogrammar' approach to analysing phraseology and collocation in ESP texts. *ASp, 59*, 5–23.

Gledhill, C., & Kübler, N. (2016). What can linguistic approaches bring to English for specific purposes. *ASp, 69*, 65–95.

Gnazzo, P. J. (2011). The chief ethics and compliance officer: A test of endurance. *Business and Society Review, 116*, 533–553.

Goffman, E. (1967). *Interaction ritual: Essays on face-to-face interaction.* Oxford: Aldine.

Grafström, M., & Windell, K. (2011). The role of infomediaries: CSR in the business press during 2000–2009. *Journal of Business Ethics, 103*, 221.

Greenwood, R., Suddaby, R., & Hinings, C. R. (2002). Theorizing change: The role of professional associations in the transformation of institutionalized fields. *Academy of Management Journal, 45*, 58–80.

Gumperz, J. J. (1982). *Discourse strategies.* Cambridge: Cambridge University Press.

Gunnarsson, B.-L., Linell, P., & Nordberg, B. (Eds.). (2014). *The construction of professional discourse.* Routledge.

Hall, C., Sarangi, S., & Slembrouck, S. (2014). Moral construction in social work discourse. In B.-L. Gunnarsson, P. Linell, & B. Nordberg (Eds.), *The construction of professional discourse* (pp. 265–291). London and New York: Routledge.

Hellgren, B., Löwstedt, J., Puttonen, L., Tienari, J., Vaara, E., & Werr, A. (2002). How issues become (re) constructed in the media: Discursive practices in the AstraZeneca merger. *British Journal of Management, 13*, 123–140.

Hoffman, R. (1985). Some implications of metaphor for philosophy and psychology of science. In *The ubiquity of metaphor* (pp. 327–380). John Benjamins.

Huntington, M. J. (1956). *Sociology of professions, 1945–55.* Sociology in the United States of America, Paris, UNESCO.

Hydén, L.-C. (2014). The institutional narrative as drama. In B.-L. Gunnarsson, P. Linell, & B. Nordberg (Eds.), *The construction of professional discourse* (pp. 245–264). London and New York: Routledge.

Isani, S. (2004). Compétence de culture professionnelle: définition, degrés et didactisation. *ASp, 43–44*, 5–21.

Jacobs, G. (1999). Self-reference in press releases. *Journal of Pragmatics, 31*, 219–242.

Lazzeretti, C. (2016). Exhibition press announcements: An evolving or dissolving genre? In G. M. Alessi & G. Jacobs (Eds.), *The ins and outs of business and professional discourse research* (pp. 204–224). London: Palgrave Macmillan.

Lønsmann, D. (2016). Negotiating positionality in ethnographic investigations of workplace settings: Student, consultant or confidante? In G. M. Alessi & G. Jacobs (Eds.), *The ins and outs of business and professional discourse research* (pp. 13–36). London: Palgrave Macmillan.

MacColl, J. (1997). The professional magazine and parallel publishing. *D-Lib Magazine, 3–2.* Retrieved from http://dlib.org/dlib/february97/02maccoll.html

Mémet, M., & Hillion, L. (2004). Éditorial. *ASp, 43–44*, 1–3.
Miller, C. R. (1984). Genre as social action. *Quarterly Journal of Speech, 70*, 151–167.
Millot, P. (2019). Retrieving the specialised substance from a corpus of professional discourse in the field of records and information management. *ASp, 76*, 49–70.
Mishler, E. G. (2014). The interactional construction of narratives in medical and life-history interviews. In B.-L. Gunnarsson, P. Linell, & B. Nordberg (Eds.), *The construction of professional discourse* (pp. 223–244). London and New York: Routledge.
Nijholt, J. J., Heusinkveld, S., & Benders, J. (2014). Handling management ideas: Gatekeeping, editors and professional magazines. *Scandinavian Journal of Management, 30*, 470–484.
Peffers, K., & Ya, T. (2003). Identifying and evaluating the universe of outlets for information systems research: Ranking the journals. *Journal of Information Technology Theory and Application, 5*, 6.
Percebois, J. (2006). Les communautés discursives à l'interface du linguistique et du disciplinaire. *Langues et cultures: une histoire d'interface*, 67–89.
Petit, M. (2010). Le discours spécialisé et le spécialisé du discours: Repères pour l'analyse du discours en anglais de spécialité. E-rea. *Revue électronique d'études sur le monde anglophone 8–1*. https://doi.org/10.4000/erea.1400.
Peynaud, C. (2015). Les mots du journalisme: de la terminologie à la culture professionnelle. *ASp, 68*, 25–44.
Rayson, P. (2008). From key words to key semantic domains. *International Journal of Corpus Linguistics, 13*, 519–549.
Resche, C. (1999). De l'utilité d'une approche syntaxique en langue spécialisée: exemple de l'anglais économique. *ASp. la revue du GERAS*, (23–26), 121–138.
Resche, C. (2003). Décryptage d'un genre particulier: Les communiqués de presse de la Banque Centrale américaine. *ASp, 39–40*, 21–35.
Resche, C. (2013). *Economic terms and beyond: How researchers in specialised varieties of English can benefit from focusing on terms.* Berne: Peter Lang.
Resche, C. (2016). Quelques pistes pour aborder la notion d'engagement dans les domaines de l'économie, de la finance et dans le monde de l'entreprise du point de vue de la recherche en anglais de spécialité. *ASp, 70*, 107–126.
Saber, A. (2016). Editorial: Immanuel Kant and ESP's new frontier. *ASp, 69*, 1–6.
Sacks, H. (1972). An initial investigation of the usability of conversational data for doing sociology. In D. Sudnow (Ed.), *Studies in social interaction* (pp. 31–73). New York: The Free Press.
Saks, M. (2012). Defining a profession: The role of knowledge and expertise. *Professions and Professionalism*, 2–1. https://doi.org/10.7577/pp.v2i1.151.

Sampson, S. (2016). The "right way": moral capitalism and the emergence of the corporate ethics and compliance officer. *Journal of Business Anthropology*, 65–86.
Scott, M., & Tribble, C. (2006). *Textual patterns: Key words and corpus analysis in language education* (Vol. 22). Amsterdam and New York: John Benjamins Publishing.
Stubbs, M. (2010). Three concepts of keywords. *Keyness in Texts*, 21–42.
Swales, J. (1996). Occluded genres in the academy: The case of the submission letter. In E. Ventola & A. Mauranen (Eds.), *Academic writing* (pp. 45–58). Amsterdam and New York: John Benjamins Publishing.
Swales, J. (2016). Reflections on the concept of discourse community. *ASp, 69*, 7–19.
Torstendahl, R. (2005). The need for a definition of 'profession'. *Current Sociology, 53*, 947–951.
Vaara, E., Tienari, J., & Laurila, J. (2006). Pulp and paper fiction: On the discursive legitimation of global industrial restructuring. *Organization Studies, 27*, 789–813.
Van Der Yeught, M. (2016). A proposal to establish epistemological foundations for the study of specialised languages. *ASp, 69*, 41–63.
Van Der Yeught, M. (2017). L'étude de cas en anglais financier et ses fondements théoriques. *Les Langues Modernes*. Retrieved from https://hal.archives-ouvertes.fr/hal-01632980
Van Der Yeught, M. (2018). Studying the diachronic dimension of specialised languages through an intentional approach to their social ontology. *Textes et contextes*, 13. Retrieved from http://preo.u-bourgogne.fr/textesetcontextes/index.php?id=2329
Vergne, J.-P. (2011). Toward a new measure of organizational legitimacy: Method, validation, and illustration. *Organizational Research Methods, 14*, 484–502.
Wierzbicka, A. (1997). *Understanding cultures through their key-words*. Oxford: Oxford University Press.
Wolf, J., & Rosenberg, T. (2012). How individual scholars can reduce the rigor-relevance gap in management research. *Business Research, 5*, 178–196.
Zavyalova, A., Pfarrer, M., Reger, R. K., & Shapiro, D. L. (2012). Managing the message: The effects of firm actions and industry spillovers on media coverage following wrongdoing. *Academy of Management Journal, 55*, 1079–1101.

4

Researching Trust in Business Partnerships: Reflections on Data Collection and Positionality

Christina Efthymiadou

Introduction

This chapter focuses on two core concepts that concern workplace researchers, namely linguistic authenticity and researcher's positioning. In discussing these concepts, I draw and reflect on personal experience of working on my PhD project. The doctoral project under discussion is now completed and examined the discursive construction and performance of trust between Greek and Turkish business partners involved in cross-border collaboration. The project sought to capture the ways in which trustworthiness is understood, warranted and performed by participants and adopted an ethnographic approach. It included 56 hours of semi-structured ethnographic interviews with business partners from seven SMEs and audio and video recordings of natural interaction including formal meetings, dinners, visits and everyday talk. The data were

C. Efthymiadou (✉)
Bristol Business School, Bristol, UK
e-mail: christina.efthymiadou@uwe.ac.uk

G. Jacobs, S. Decock (eds.), *Good Data in Business and Professional Discourse Research and Teaching*, Communicating in Professions and Organizations,
https://doi.org/10.1007/978-3-030-61757-8_4

analysed from an interactional sociolinguistic perspective. A significant part of the project focused on a specific case, a company called SforSteel (pseudonym), the founders of which granted me permission to participate in and record their everyday interactions. In what follows, I mainly reflect on and discuss my experience from two fieldtrips in Turkey, where I accompanied Nick, my Greek informant for the SforSteel case, and observed and recorded his interactions with his Turkish partners.

The first part of the chapter focuses on the concept of linguistic authenticity and its implications for data collection in professional discourse research. After offering an overview of the discussions in the field, I explain my own position and the way it influenced the data collection process in my project. My analysis provides support to the view that interview data can indeed be a legitimate and valuable source of information in ethnographic projects, despite the influence of the researcher's presence on the interaction at hand. With relation to the book's objectives, this part of the chapter feeds into the discussion on what counts as authentic data in professional discourse research.

In the second part of the chapter I turn to the concept of researcher's positioning, discussing how perceptions of the researcher impact the research process and the data collected. More specifically, I discuss how personal characteristics of the researcher affect access to data and relationships with the research subjects, drawing always on my own research experience. The chapter adopts the viewpoint that the ethnographic researcher is an active participant in the research process and this should not be perceived as compromising the value of the research findings. Workplace researchers should reflect on their effect on the research process and account for it in their work. Discussing researcher's positioning is viewed as closely related to questions about the ultimate quality of the data collected and the research findings' rigor.

Linguistic Authenticity and Data Collection

Sociolinguistic research has long been concerned with authenticity, or what is often referred to as 'real language', meaning language that is produced by authentic speakers in authentic communicative situations

(Bucholtz 2003). Although authenticity seems to critically affect the research process, influencing the way sociolinguists choose their research topics and participants, as well as the ways they collect and analyse their data, it is rarely a topic of discussion in its own right (ibid.). Here, I discuss how authenticity underwrites workplace discourse studies and how it affected my methodological choices in my doctoral research project.

Authenticity has critically influenced the work of workplace discourse analysts for at least the last 30 years. Studies in the field focus on what is often known as "naturally occurring speech" (see Bucholtz 2003, p. 406), meaning by this interactions that unfold as part of the everyday life of people and not as a result of pre-arranged conditions (Hutchby and Wooffitt 1998). Considering the above, professional discourse research often involves the recording and analysis of job meetings, transactional interactions or small talk instances at work in an attempt to discover how people create meaning, and construct and negotiate roles and identities in workplace communication (Angouri and Marra 2011; Baxter 2010).

Discussions on authenticity often bring to the forefront concerns about the role of the linguist as an "obstacle to linguistic authenticity" (Bucholtz 2003, p. 406) or what is more widely known as the observer's paradox (Labov 1972; Sarangi 2007). The observer's paradox refers to situations where the presence of the researcher in a setting affects the way the phenomenon unfolds; it suggests that if the participants know they are being observed, they would not act in a natural way (Richards 2003) and would not use language in the way they would if they interacted only with community insiders (Bucholtz 2003). By insisting on the study of naturally occurring data, scholars attempt to minimize the effects that their presence could have on the views and stances expressed and thus minimize the biases included in the dataset (Bucholtz 2003; Potter and Hepburn 2005; Silverman 2001).

Sociolinguists have positioned themselves in different ways in relation to authenticity and the legitimacy of certain types of data, such as those emerging from interviews and focus groups (see Edley and Litosseliti 2010). A part of discourse analysts, especially conversation analysts, have traditionally insisted on the importance of collecting naturally occurring data that unfold as part of the normal every-day business of participants, often referred to as actual data, raising methodological concerns about the validity of data stemming from interviews and focus groups. The underlying argument for this position is that interview and focus-group data are dependent on the interviewer's and moderator's stances, as it is them who invite the participants in the first place and set the agenda for the discussion afterwards, while their contributions can lead the interviewees in prescribed directions/topics/answers (Potter and Hepburn 2005). In this respect, data stemming from interviews or focus groups are considered to be contrived and compromised (Speer 2002), or 'manufactured' as put by Silverman (2001). Interview and focus-group data then, according to Potter (1996), should be used only in cases where the researcher is interested in these forums per se, for example in meaning-making processes in interviews/focus groups. In a similar vein, he argues that social scientists should be able to apply the 'dead scientist's test' in order to assess the appropriateness of their research data, meaning that naturally occurring data should emerge from social interactions that would have happened even if the researcher who was supposed to gather them was somehow unexpectedly killed before collecting them (Potter 1996).

In recent years, the above views have been forcefully criticised by discourse analysts, who argue for the de facto situated character of discourse data. According to Edley and Litosseliti (2010), the very distinction between natural and contrived data seems to be problematic from a discourse analytical point of view, considering that discourse analysts have long been on the forefront of showing how all discourse data is indexical or context-specific. From this perspective, all discourse data is affected by the social context in which it was produced and hence it is 'got up' for something. Consequently, interview and focus-group data do not seem to be more compromised or contrived than any other data set stemming from recordings of 'natural' talk. After all, even in situations where participants record interactions without being around (as when they provide recorders to participants to record themselves), the researcher's influence is not absent from the research process (Angouri 2018). In a similar vein, Bucholtz (2003, p. 406) argues that all research situations, even those designed by conversation analysts with minimal presence of the researcher, are only "approximations to 'authentic' (non-research) contexts of language use", since prior consent from participants is required in all cases. Bucholtz (2003, p. 406) concludes that "if our goal is truly to collect and analyse authentic speech, then we are doomed to failure—or to extremely unethical research practice that no sociolinguist would endorse".

Interviews as Constructed Events

With regards to interview data in particular, contemporary thinking in the field highlights the importance of understanding and treating interviews as two-way exchanges between the researcher and the interviewee (Edley and Litosseliti 2010; Holliday 2012; Kvale 2007) who are both agents in the interactional event (Angouri 2018). Interviews, in this context, are conceptualised as "social practice" (Talmy 2011, p. 27) and interview data are collaboratively produced by the researcher and interviewee and cannot therefore be considered contaminated or compromised. This perspective aligns with earlier criticisms of standard assumptions about interviewing backed by the seminal work of Holstein and Gubrium (1995), who drew on social constructionist insights that described language as a way of acting in the world and talked about interviews as knowledge building processes. They further suggested that the interviewer and interviewee are involved in meaning-making processes when they interact in the context of interviews. In that context, the informant should not be perceived as a "repository of knowledge that awaits to be discovered by the interviewer, but as a constructor of knowledge alongside interviewers" (Holstein and Gubrium 1995, p. 4). In practice, the adoption of such a view implies that the researcher should treat interviews not only as the products of what people say, but also of how and why they say it; in other words, researchers should simultaneously discern between and pay attention to the referential and performative aspects of discourse (Freeman 1993; Mishler 1986; Talmy 2011).

Based on the above, real authentic data, meaning data not produced in the context of a research setting, would be not ethically sound. From this perspective, interviews, perceived as a collaborative achievement, are a legitimate and valuable source of information and should not be abolished from sociolinguists' toolkit for the sake of authenticity. Interview data can indeed provide useful insights in terms of how and why people say things, while they can also be used as a complementary source of data alongside other methods. For example, retrospective interviews can be used to shed light on participants' understandings of recorded events. In a similar vein, Angouri (2018) talks about the usefulness of involving participants in the analysis of recorded data, by having follow-up interviews with them to find out their understanding of 'what is going on' in the recorded event. In such interviews, the participants are shown the transcripts of selected excerpts by the researcher and they are asked to offer their account on the event. Such interviews allow participants to bring their perspectives and contextual knowledge in the analysis and are considered valuable for interpreting the events.

With regards to the project discussed here, I align with the latter group of discourse analysts and I adopt the view of Peräkylä (2005) that the two types of data—researcher provoked and naturally occurring—should be perceived as a continuum rather than as a dichotomy. For the purposes of my project, I adopted the view of interviews as situated action (Cicourel 1964) and social practice (Talmy 2011). The project included 20 semi-structured interviews, which were perceived as interactive encounters between the participants and me, and my contribution to them was treated as a key part of the data and as affecting the development of the discussion (Richards et al. 2012). The project included also recordings of naturally occurring interactions; formal and informal meetings between partners, small talk at work and social gatherings were audio and, when possible, video recorded. However, these were treated in my project as a source of data that sheds light on different dimensions of doing trust rather than as a more appropriate data source than interviews. Different data offer different lenses for studying the phenomena of interest and allow for a more holistic understanding (see Schnurr and Zayts 2017). Moreover, rich and diverse datasets point out connections between the different insights and identify patterns that future research could address in more detail (Angouri 2018). In the context of my project, thus, the different datasets were treated as shedding light on different dimensions of the phenomenon studied and informed each other in the interpretation of how trust is enacted in the studied context. More specifically, interviews were initially analysed to identify the different factors that participants perceived as affecting perceptions of trustworthiness in the given context. Successively, interactional data was analysed to see how the above factors were made relevant and discursively performed in everyday interactions (dinner talk, meeting talk) by the same participants.

To illustrate how interviews can indeed be a valid tool for social research and offer valuable insights for the phenomena studied, I hereby draw on interview data from my project. More specifically, in what follows I present and analyse an excerpt drawn from one of the first interviews with Nick, a Greek participant, in his office in Greece. I chose to discuss this excerpt as it is a prime example of how my presence affected the way the discussion between me and Nick unfolded, but still offers valuable insights about Nick's positioning and self-representation. On top of that, this particular interview proved valuable for making sense of my observation logs, demonstrating how interviews can be used to complement other data collection methods.

Excerpt 1

Context: This excerpt is drawn from the first interview I had with Nick, in his office in Greece. The office walls were full of photographs and souvenirs from his trips and Nick was talking me through some of them. In this excerpt Nick focuses on a scarf that hangs on the wall. The conversation took place in the Greek language.

Original transcript in Greek

(1)	Nick	Αν σε ρωτήσουν εκεί πέρα τι γράφει εκείνο το κασκολάκι
(2)	Res	Α, ναι τι γράφει;
(3)	Nick	Bize heryer Trabzon. Που σημαίνει για εμάς όπου είμαστε είναι
(4)		Τραπεζούντα.
(5)	Res	Πωπω
(6)	Nick	Είναι σύνθημα των φιλάθλων της Τραπεζούντας. Το ίδιο πράγμα,
(7)		το ίδιο λογότυπο, το έχω στις πινακίδες του αυτοκινήτου μου.
(8)	Res	Απίστευτο.
(9)	Nick	Αν βγεις έξω και φωτογραφίσεις το αυτοκίνητό μου,
(10)		είναι πίσω, στις πινακίδες.
(11)	Res	Από την Τραπεζούντα είστε;
(12)	Nick	Η μια οικογένεια είναι από εκεί. Της μάνας μου είναι
(13)		από την Τραπεζούντα, η άλλη είναι από την Κερασούντα.

English translation

(1)	Nick	If they ask you what is written on that scarf...
(2)	Res	Oh, yes. What does it mean?
(3)	Nick	Bize Heryer Trabzon (turkish). Which means for us wherever we
(4)		Are it is Trabzon.
(5)	Res	Oh...
(6)	Nick	It is the motto of the supporters of Trabzon. The same thing,
(7)		The same motto, is written in my registration plate.
(8)	Res	Unbelievable
(9)	Nick	If you go out and take a photo of my car, it is below the
(10)		Registration plate
(11)	Res	So you are from Trabzon?
(12)	Nick	The one family yes. My mother's is from Trabzon. The other
(13)		From Giresun.

This excerpt is significant for its performative rather than referential dimension of discourse (Freeman 1993; Mishler 1986). Nick points out to me the things he would like me to pay attention to (lines 1, 7, 9, 10) which is significant as a practice on its own. This is the first time we meet and Nick performs an identity for me and decides which parts of himself to foreground. I am aware that he is foregrounding a specific regional identity of a person who comes from Trabzon and can be described as Pontic (denoting people who come from the Black Sea area of modern Turkey) more strongly, because I informed him that I am interested in identity issues in workplace contexts. I am aware that the observer's paradox becomes relevant at this point; my presence and particular research interests influence the way Nick acts in front of me and the identity he foregrounds. If I had not mentioned that I am looking at identity issues in the given context, Nick might have not even bothered to talk me through the slogan written on his scarf and car signs. Following the discussion on authenticity, a discourse analyst in search of real authentic data, would consider this excerpt probably as compromised or contaminated and would not bother with analyzing it. Yet, the fact that Nick decides to overplay this identity for me, conveys meaning and is analytically significant for making sense of the given context. Nick wants to be perceived as Pontic and works hard and systematically to achieve this interactionally. He intentionally puts emphasis on the fact that the slogan associated with the people coming from the particular area, and its regional football team called Trabzonspor, is featured on his car signs (lines 7, 9, 10). In this way, he makes a strong identity claim for himself as a person who identifies with the specific slogan and hence with the specific regional group. Nick places symbolic significance on his Pontic group membership and the fact that the particular slogan is displayed on his car signs acts as an index of this identity.

The photo of his car that Nick refers to here was subsequently sent to me by Nick himself (for a snapshot of the photo see Fig. 4.1).

What seems more interesting is the fact that, according to my observation notes, Nick was showing the same photo and performing the Pontic identity to a number of other people while on business trips in Turkey. More specifically, he was displaying the same photo of his car to the people he was meeting during an exhibition and at a regional club we visited while at fieldwork. All these people belonged to the same regional group, identifying themselves as Pontics. Being part of this regional group was of paramount importance in this context. The specific identity was shared between partners of this case-study and defined their relationship and ways of doing business and trust in multiple ways. Partners' shared

Fig. 4.1 Snapshot of the registration plate of Nick's car

identification as Pontics affected also the way I was perceived by them. I will not expand further on this here, but will reflect on it in the following section when discussing access issues.

Going back to the data, although it is apparent that Nick's contribution in the excerpt above is guided by my interest in identity issues, the performance of the particular identity by Nick for me is still analytically significant and provides valuable insights for the way he wants to be perceived and the significance of this identity in the given context. Even more importantly, what the above discussion shows in relation to the book's focus, is that interview data can indeed be a legitimate and valuable source of data in professional discourse research. The influence and contributions of the researcher in the interactions should not be penalized and ignored or perceived as creating bias in the data, but on the contrary recognized and taken into consideration in the analysis. The researcher in this context should be perceived as another participant, an active agent of the event, whose contributions are equally valid and deserve analysis. Moreover, interview data can inform the interpretation of other sources of data, such as observation logs and photos, by shedding light on participants' interpretations and understandings of the observed/recorded events.

Still discussing data-related issues, the next part of the chapter focuses on another concept that is closely related to debates on authenticity and researcher's influence in the research process and the ultimate type and 'quality' of the data collected, namely researcher's positioning. Similarly to the first section, I will first present an overview of the main discussions about it in the field before moving on to reflect on my own experience.

Researcher's Positioning

Perceptions of the Researcher and Consequences for the Research

Following the discussion above, researchers form part of the research process, affecting the way interactions unfold. From this perspective, discussions on data authenticity should also involve reflection on the role of the researcher in the research process and more specifically on the ways the researcher is perceived by participants. Researcher's positioning is important in all research that involves data interpretation, but acquires particular significance in ethnographic projects, like the one discussed here, which involve most of the times some participant observation. Participant observation is one of the main sources of data in ethnographic research and requires the ethnographer to spend time with the research participants and gather data through her lived experience of interacting with them (Hammersley and Atkinson 2007). In this way she gains insights about things participants forget or avoid mentioning and is in a better position to interpret things in the ways she does (Emerson et al. 1995; O'Reilly 2009). Participant observation offers the researcher the chance to see directly actual behaviours of participants and allows her to gather contextual information for the settings in which the studied phenomenon takes place (Dornyei 2007). This information can then critically support the interpretations of other data collected.

A common theme that arises in discussions about ethnographic observation is the multifaceted role of the researcher (Hammersley and Atkinson 2007). Personal characteristics of the researcher, which among others include gender, race, personal experiences, beliefs, emotional responses to participants, can affect the positionality of the researcher and impact the research process in three main ways (Berger 2015).

First, they affect access to the field. Negotiating access to business settings is one of the most traditional challenges that professional discourse scholars face (Alessi and Jacobs 2016). Some communities are easy to gain access to, but others might resist their opening/exposure to the researcher even when she is already part of the given community (Hammersley and Atkinson 2007). For example, if a researcher happens to be part of a certain group (a specific sports club, professional association), this does not mean that members of the given group would be happy to speak out about their experiences in relation to a particular issue. In cases where the researcher has no connections with the desired community, it is common to make use of gatekeepers (Richards et al. 2012). Even in that case, though, issues of access and common understanding need to be negotiated between the researcher and participants all the way through the research process (Alessi and Jacobs 2016; Hammersley and Atkinson 2007). As Hammersley and Atkinson (2007) argue, gaining access can be described as a full-time occupation and access rights might need to be renegotiated even after months into the fieldwork. They bring up as an example the case of Barbera-Stein's (1979) research in therapeutic or daycare centres for preschool children, where she was denied access to a set of puppet-play therapeutic sessions even after eight months of fieldwork, while she was allowed to record interactional data with families which she thought would be more sensitive. By discussing her case, they conclude that while researchers need to remain sensitive to issues of access within the same context, they should also allow for flexibility in the research process and be prepared to overcome their own presuppositions regarding what is accessible and what it is not. Another factor that impacts access is establishing common understanding between researcher and practitioners. Alessi and Jacobs (2016) argue that one of the biggest obstacles in gaining access to data is the lack of common ground between practitioners and professional discourse researchers. Researchers are often seen by practitioners as ignoring their know-how and using meta-language and terminology that is inaccessible to them, making the research outputs alien and irrelevant to their interests. To overcome this challenge, it is important for researchers and practitioners to agree on a common plan of action, which brings together academic insights and practitioners' know-how (ibid.).

At a second level, personal characteristics of the researcher shape the nature of the researcher-researched relationship which successively affects the information that participants are willing to disclose. In cases where participants develop a close trusting relationship with the researcher, they are more willing to share their experiences with them (Berger 2015). This can become particularly relevant in cases where participants are asked to share sensitive information about themselves. For example, in a study investigating sexual harassment at work, a female victim might feel comfortable sharing her experience with a female researcher.

Last, the researcher's background determines the choice of the lens through which she filters and makes meaning of the data, shaping thus the findings and conclusions of the study (see Kacen and Chaitin 2006).

There are certainly many different readings to the data of an ethnographic project and the personal history and identity of the researcher plays a crucial role in determining which one will prevail (Angouri 2018). For a reading to be legitimate, one needs to take into consideration participants' perspectives and also account for/reflect on the effect of their own background on the data interpretation. In what follows, I discuss and reflect on my own background and the way it affected my field experience.

Negotiating Access to the Field

In the case of the present project, the role of gatekeepers was critical for accessing the field. Different people and institutions acted as gatekeepers at different stages of the data collection process. First, I approached some companies through the help of the Turkish-Greek Commercial Chamber of Thessaloniki, which provided me with company names and contact details. My first attempt of recruiting companies proved unfruitful and at a later stage, I used some family contacts to get in touch with the founder of a transportation company, who then put me in touch with other companies which had cross-border activities with Turkey, such as SforSteel, the company which became my case study. The founder of that transportation company acted as my gatekeeper in the initial stage of recruiting participants, while the founder of SforSteel then acted as my gatekeeper during my trips to Turkey and helped me to gain access to places and interactions that would have been very difficult to attend without his help. Throughout the process of negotiating access, I had to adjust my research plan multiple times.

The selection of the particular topic, my presence in the field and the lens through which I filtered the interactions observed, have also been affected by a factor that deserves acknowledgment and reflection, my Greek background. I was born and have lived most of my life in the northern part of Greece, in the city of Thessaloniki. My family, although not entirely, does have a small percentage of refugee background since my paternal great-grandparents moved to Greece as refugees from the broader area of the Black Sea region. Although my ancestors had never identified themselves as Pontics, and nor do I, their family trip to Greece and sufferings have made me familiar with the specific context and attentive to the stories of these people. This background spurred my interest for researching the Greco-Turkish context and affected my heightened attention to the personal stories of the SforSteel participants and the way I read them.

At the same time, my background played an important role for the way I was perceived by the research participants. Nick in our first interaction over the phone assumed that I had Pontic origin like him, due to the ending of my surname, which denotes an association with the area (it is common for Greek surnames to denote origin). In our first meeting, he showed interest and asked me about my background and was touched by the fact that my great grand-parents moved to Greece as refugees from the broader Black Sea area during the Greco-Turkish war in 1919. Although I made clear to him that my ancestors did not self-identity as Pontics and I had no attachment to this specific identity myself, when he subsequently introduced me to his partners, he described me as 'a girl of ours', projecting the specific regional identity to me, which contributed to being perceived in a positive light by them. Interestingly, over the course of fieldwork, I started to develop attachment with the Pontic identity and I got involved also in some of the cultural activities my participants were involved in, such as regional dancing.

My family background played an important role for gaining the trust of Nick and his partners. Following insights from previous studies, this could be interpreted by the fact that shared group membership acts as a 'basis for presumptive trust' (Kramer and Lewicki 2010; Loh et al. 2010) and serves for "defining the boundaries of low risk interpersonal trust that bypass the need for personal knowledge" (Brewer 1981, p. 356). This is based on the presupposition that in-group members tend to attribute positive characteristics to fellow group members, such as honesty, cooperativeness and trustworthiness (Brewer 1996), which leads to a depersonalised type of trust towards them (Kramer and Lewicki 2010).

All in all, my personal background played a crucial role in securing access to the field. Recruiting participants proved to be time consuming and dictated continuous plan adjustments. Once in the field, identity issues became relevant again, impacting the research process in multiple ways. I discuss this in the next section.

Balancing Between Different Researcher Roles

Apart from access negotiation, researcher's positioning impacts the fieldwork experience in multiple ways, shaping the focus of observation as well as the relationship with participants who might perceive the researcher in different ways. While in the field, ethnographers need to negotiate their identity on a constant basis. At different stages of the research process, the participants might perceive them as insiders, outsiders, agents of change, overhearers, depending on their level of participation and relationship with them (Sarangi 2002). Further complexity is added also from the twofold role of the researcher as participant and observer. As O'Reilly (2009) notes, participant observation includes two key elements: participation and observation. This combination, she argues, can be a challenging one since it requires from the researcher on the one hand to become part of the community under study and involved in activities with the people observed and on the other to be an outsider to the community, watching and listening to what others do and say (ibid.). The ethnographer, then, needs to balance these two roles.

Linking this to my own experience, once in the field, I was sometimes fully participating in activities and interactions with the participants, while at other times I was either partially involved or just observing their interactions. Hence, my role was continuously shifting between that of the insider and outsider observer (O'Reilly 2009; Sarangi and Hall 1997). There were also certain moments that were impossible to pinpoint in terms of what type of observer I was. For example, in the following excerpt, drawn from the recording of every-day interaction between Nick and his Turkish and Greek partners, my role cannot be clearly defined.

Excerpt 2

Context: This excerpt is drawn from an every-day interaction between Nick and his partners in an exhibition in Istanbul. The participants are in a small room at the backstage of the exhibition stand of the SforSteel company. The participants used to spend considerable time in this room chatting informally with each other, preparing their drinks and eating. In this excerpt, Yannis, Mehmet and Nick are setting up a table for lunch and since the room is quite small, they negotiate who is going to sit down in the few chairs and who is going to be standing.

Original transcript with a mixture of Greek and English including mixture of Greek and English languages

(1) Yannis Που θα στέκεσαι; Ορθά; Όχι κάτσε κάτω ρε!(reg dialect and Greek)
(2) Mhm Yannis, Yannis… (English)
(3) Yannis Since 6 o'clock you are here (English)
(4) Mhm Yes ok, that's fine. This is different. (English)
(5) Nick Αν ακούω Πόντιο ρε πούστη με Πόντιο να μιλάνε αγγλικά
(6) τρελαίνομαι. (Greek)
(7) Yiannis Εμείς πάντα με τον Mehmet σκαλώναμε τα Ποντικά, Ρούμτζα,
(8) Και μετά, εγγλέζε… τι να κάνω ρε φίλε. (Greek)
(9) Nick Χριστίνα φέρε ένα ποτήρι από 'κει ρε… (Greek)

Translated text

(1) Yannis Where are you going to stand? Still? No, sit down!
(2) Mhm Yannis, yannis…
(3) Yannis Since 6 o'clock you are here
(4) Mhm Yes ok, that's fine. This is different.
(5) Nick When I listen to Pontic people speaking in English with each
(6) Other I go crazy man.
(7) Yiannis With Mehmet whenever we face difficulties speaking Pontic we
(8) Switch to English… what can I do man…
(9) Nick Christina bring a glass from there…

In the excerpt above, my role could not be clearly defined as participant/insider or non-participant/outsider observer. The research subjects are aware of my presence in the room, but they do not involve me in the interaction, which is centred on linguistic practices related to the regional group they belong to. However, they are aware of my presence in the room and Nick makes a request to pass him a glass for his friend (line 9). In cases like this, my presence does not go unnoticed; yet, my role and contributions are peripheral to the main interactional event and could not be perceived as influencing the way the interaction unfolds. This blurriness has been reported as a common issue among researchers. As Morse and Richard (2002) suggest, the dichotomy between participant/ insider, non-participant/ outsider observer is not clear-cut and oversimplifies the whole process of watching and listening. Morse and Richard (2002) also argue that all ethnographic observation involves at least some participation. In a similar vein, Lønsmann (2016) argues that ethnographic researchers are not supposed to be neutral observers but are part of the research process and their relationship with participants should be a point of reflection.

Language and Gender Considerations

My experience in the field was heavily impacted by my gender and language proficiency. While in the field I could not absorb everything; rather I focused on specific interactions and relationships (Emerson et al. 1995). For most of the time on fieldtrips in Turkey, I was shadowing Nick, my Greek participant. I stayed close to him, following him in activities and observing his interactions with his Turkish partners. I was particularly interested in the topics they were talking about and the general climate that existed in the room when they were together. Nick acted as my main informant in most of the cases, providing me with translations/summaries of the topics discussed or with background information to make sense of the interactions. The choice of staying close to Nick was primarily guided by my research focus but was also the result of the fact that I only had a very basic knowledge of Turkish and was unfamiliar with the context, and also that most of the Turkish participants did not speak English. The fact that I could only partly communicate with Turkish participants played an important role in my feelings at initial stages of the research process and had an effect on the intimacy of the relationship I developed with them. As time went by though, I became more comfortable with the context. With some of the Turkish participants we even managed to communicate using my basic Turkish and their use of a regional dialect. In some situations, partners communicated in the dialect of the Pontic region. I was able to understand most of these interactions as I was familiar with some of the words through contact with people speaking it during my childhood years and due to the fact that the dialect is based on ancient Greek language. Due to the particularities of the context discussed above, observation was of paramount importance for making sense of the data. My presence in the field and the chance to observe the partners' style and tone when talking, but also their body posture and the general climate of the interaction, was invaluable for overcoming the language barrier and for making sense of their interactions (Dornyei 2007), which then added insight into the translated text.

My limited skills in the Turkish language had practical implications in terms of communication and also caused feelings of insecurity at certain moments, especially when I found myself in spaces and events attended only by men, such as a regional club where my participants used to spend their evenings socialising with other people coming from their region. The particular club was always very busy and I often found myself alone with 50 middle aged Turkish men around me. Also, as my main informant told me, the wives of these men are not allowed within the club, so watching a young strange woman around was something new for them. My presence in places like this, where women are not normally allowed, did not go unnoticed and I often felt the attention on my face (see also Lønsmann 2016 on female researcher identity). In a few cases, I also realised that Nick was being interrogated by other men about his choice of bringing me to these places. On my first trip, this was more obvious, as I was regarded with suspicion. On my second trip, all of the partners were more comfortable with my presence, so most of these challenges were no longer an issue. In any case, being accompanied by my main informant, the Greek partner of the SforSteel case, made me feel protected.

An interesting point in relation to my gender identity, is the fact that SforSteel participants used to refer to me as "the girl" while in the field. My main informant introduced me like this to his partners while we were in our first meeting. More specifically he said: "I have a girl of ours here doing some research on…" and this was the way I was referred to in their discussions. During my first fieldtrip to Turkey, where I was accompanied by my partner in life as well, they kept referring to both of us as "παιδιά", which literally translated means 'kids' but is also used as meaning 'lads/young people'. The following excerpt illustrates this point:

Excerpt 3

Context: This excerpt is drawn from an every-day interaction between Nick and his partner Mehmet, who discuss their schedule for the next day.

Original transcript including mixture of the regional dialect, Greek and Turkish language

(1)	Nick	Λοιπόν, αύριο το ίτο σο ίτο. Τι ώρα να πάμε; (reg dialect)
(2)	Mhm	πιο ύστερα. On iki bir να φεύγουμε (Greek and Turksih)
(3)	Nick	Δώδεκα-μία η ώρα. Cuma είναι η Παρασκευή. Λοιπόν να έχουμε
(4)		τα **παιδιά** μετ'εμάς. Μόνο αβούτο το ραντεβού έχουμε; (Greek and regional dialect)
(5)	Mhm	Και να πάμε το ίτο το τεμέτερον, μπορούμε να το δεις με το προγκραμ (Greek and regional dialect)

Translated text

(1)	Nick	So tomorrow we are going there. What time shall we say;
(2)	Mhm	Late. Around 12 or 1 o'clock to leave.
(3)	Nick	12–1 o'clock. Cuma is Friday. We are going to have the
(4)		**Kids/lads** with us too. Is this our only appointment?
(5)	Mhm	And we shall take our own laptop so that you can use the software

In the above excerpt Nick refers to me and my partner as paidia, meaning kids or lads (line 4). Work from a conversation analytic approach, more specifically, basic principles of membership categorization analysis (MCA) as developed by Sacks (1992), becomes relevant in this context. MCA studies the way people make sense of their world by making categorisations and attributions. Membership categories are meaning-making resources as the classification of a person to a category provides ways to interpret, classify and assign meaning to actions and utterances (Sacks 1992). Being cast in a category thus provides a warrant for further inferences. The label 'girl' in this context is associated with certain characteristics, i.e. being a young female person, often vested with a sense of naivety and minimal power. The label 'lads/young people' is associated with similar characteristics. Although at first the attribution of these labels sounded as challenging my professional identity as a researcher working in a highly-esteemed research institution, it nevertheless benefited the study, since participants did not feel intimidated by my presence and allowed me to access places where I would not have been welcomed under another capacity.

As shown, issues relating to language proficiency as well as labels attached to the researcher can critically affect the way she is perceived by participants and consequently access to data rights and relationships. The role of the researcher is dynamic and perceptions can change over the course of the research process. A researcher initially viewed with suspicion can become trusted over the course of study and relationships of mutual trust can develop. Personal characteristics can also impact the data analysis stage, an issue which I discuss next.

Filtering the Data

Researcher's positioning determines also the lens through which the researcher filters and makes meaning of the data collected (Berger 2015). Reflecting back to the stage of organizing and making meaning of the collected data, the research process was affected by two main factors: my family background which caused an increased interest in personal narratives related to the regional identity and my limited proficiency in Turkish language which posed additional limitations at the stages of organising and transcribing the data gathered from SforSteel, the only company which allowed me to record their interactions. In relation to the latter, a significant challenge that I had to overcome was the translation of parts of the data. In most cases, the recordings included a mixture of Turkish, English and a regional dialect partners used, which made it very difficult to be transcribed and translated by one person. The following extract illustrates this:

Excerpt 4

Context: This excerpt is drawn from a meeting between SforSteel partners in their factory in Turkey.

Original transcript including talk in Turkish language and Pontic regional dialect

(1)	Mhm	Arabanin anahtari sende mi? (Turkish)
(2)	Boran	Alim geleyim (Turkish)

(3)	Ali	Emena ti eferes. Kurampie eferes to Mehmet. Emena ti eferes? (Dialect)
(4)	Nick	Kurampie (dialect)
(5)	Ali	Afise to, exereis, en troo kurempie. Giati ou xero nto na erxesai (dialect)
(6)	Nick	Ou xereis esu? Kai ntrepseai? Allah allah! (dialect)
(7)	Ali	Kerim exerei, Zack exerei. Giati ou xero? (dialect)
(8)	Nick	Ego kati na leo se, ego na leo se kai esu tranos eisai, na les. (dialect)
(9)	Ali	Ooo surat bir karis, niye ben bilmeyecegim de oburleri bilecek (Turkish)
Translated text		
(1)	Mhm	Are the car keys with you?
(2)	Boran	I'll go get it
(3)	Ali	What did you bring for me? You brought some cookies to Mehmet.
(4)	Nick	I brought you cookies too.
(5)	Ali	You know I don't eat those. Why I didn't know you were coming?
(6)	Nick	You didn't know? Shame on you. Allah, Allah! (Oh God!)
(7)	Ali	Kerim knew, Zack the same. Why wasn't I told?
(8)	Nick	I am telling you something and you have to spread the news
(9)	Ali	Huh, a sulky face, and why does everyone else knows but me...

In the extract above, partners use a mixture of Turkish language (lines 1, 2, 9) and Pontic dialect (lines 3–8), which was the most typical language pattern for them. I transcribed most of the material myself, but consulted a colleague with proficiency in Turkish when transcribing the parts that included an extended use of Turkish, as in the meeting talk recorded. To ensure data safety, I could not grant access to the recordings to third parties, such as transcribing companies. Instead, I asked my colleague to listen to the recordings from my computer and provide me with a translation, which I wrote down at the time. The help provided was considered invaluable for making sense of the data. However, the conditions in which this was done did not allow me to return to the recordings at later stages and check the transcriptions at certain points that did not make sense when analysing them (it would have been very time consuming for my colleague to revisit these excerpts). Due to this limitation, I had to exclude many parts of the meeting talk and include only those transcriptions which were more clear and meaningful.

As the above discussion indicates, data interpretation depends on the lens through which the researcher filters them which is shaped by the researcher's personal history and characteristics (Angouri 2018; Berger 2015). This should not be perceived as a limitation or as compromising the rigor of the research findings. Subjectivity seems to be inherent in any human enquiry (see also Hegelund 2005) and ethnographic projects do not and cannot take place in a vacuum (Angouri 2018). To enhance the quality of the research outputs, the researcher, then, should acknowledge the factors that impacted the research process and reflect on her own positioning when reporting the findings.

Concluding Remarks

In this chapter I discussed two concepts that—in spite of being pertinent to sociolinguistic research—are rarely the topic of discussion in their own right, namely linguistic authenticity and researcher's positioning. For both concepts, I reviewed the main trends in the literature and then reflected on my own experience of working on my doctoral project. With regards to linguistic authenticity, I focused on discussions between workplace scholars regarding the authenticity and legitimacy of data stemming from interviews and focus groups. After positioning myself with regards to those, I drew on data from my project to showcase how interviews, in which the researcher's presence clearly affected the interaction at hand, were treated as a legitimate source of data in my study. In the second part of the chapter, I turned to the concept of researcher positionality. Reflexivity is crucial for all stages of a research project (Bradbury-Jones 2007) and here I reflected on the effect of my positioning prior, during and after fieldwork, drawing on relevant data excerpts.

This chapter responds to the need for more reflexivity in workplace studies. Reflexivity is relevant to all research, but acquires more importance for ethnographers, who can use it to provide the reader with important contextual information to evaluate their involvement and effect in the research and hence to enhance the value and rigor of their work.

References

Alessi, G., & Jacobs, G. (2016). Reflections on the ins and outs of business and professional discourse research. In G. Alessi & G. Jacobs (Eds.), *The ins and outs of business and professional discourse research: Reflections on interacting with the workplace* (pp. 1–12). Basingstoke: Palgrave Macmillan.

Angouri, J. (2018). *Culture, discourse, and the workplace*. Abingdon, Oxford: Routledge.

Angouri, J., & Marra, M. (2011). *Constructing identities at work*. London: Palgrave.

Barbera-Stein, L. (1979). *Access negotiations: Comments on the sociology of the sociologist's knowledge*. Paper presented at the seventy-fourth annual meeting of the American Sociological Association. Boston, MA, August.

Baxter, J. (2010). Discourse-analytic approaches to text and talk. In L. Litosseliti (Ed.), *Research methods in linguistics* (pp. 117–137). London: Bloomsbury.

Berger, R. (2015). Now I see it, now I don't: Researcher's position and reflexivity in qualitative research. *Qualitative Research, 15*, 219–234.

Bradbury-Jones, C. (2007). Enhancing rigor in qualitative health research: Exploring subjectivity through Peshkin's I's. *Journal of Advanced Nursing, 59*, 290–298.

Brewer, M. B. (1981). Ethnocentrism and its role in interpersonal trust. In D. T. Campbell, M. B. Brewer, & B. E. Collins (Eds.), *Scientific inquiry and the social sciences* (pp. 354–360). New York: Jossey-Bass.

Brewer, M. B. (1996). In-group favoritism: The subtle side of intergroup discrimination. In D. M. Messick & A. E. Tenbrunsel (Eds.), *Codes of conduct: Behavioral research and business ethics* (pp. 160–171). New York: Russell Sage Found.

Bucholtz, M. (2003). *Sociolinguistic nostalgia and identity*. Oxford: Blackwell.

Cicourel, A. V. (1964). *Method and measurement in sociology*. New York: Free Press.

Dornyei, Z. (2007). *Research methods in applied linguistics*. Oxford: Oxford University Press.

Edley, N., & Litosseliti, L. (2010). Contemplating interviews and focus-groups. In L. Litosseliti (Ed.), *Research methods in linguistics* (pp. 155–179). London: Bloomsbury.

Emerson, R., Fretz, R. I., & Shaw, L. L. (1995). *Writing ethnographic fieldnotes*. Chicago: University of Chicago Press.

Freeman, M. (1993). *Rewriting the self: History, memory, narrative*. London: Routledge.

Hammersley, M., & Atkinson, P. (2007). *Ethnography: Principles in practice* (3rd ed.). New York: Routledge.
Hegelund, A. (2005). Objectivity and subjectivity in the ethnographic method. *Qualitative Health Research, 15*, 647–668.
Holliday, A. (2012). Interrogating researcher participation in an interview study of intercultural contribution in the workplace. *Qualitative Inquiry, 18*, 504–515.
Holstein, J. A., & Gubrium, J. F. (1995). *The active interview*. London: Sage.
Hutchby, I., & Wooffitt, R. (1998). *Conversation analysis: Principles, practices and applications*. Oxford: Polity Press.
Kacen, L., & Chaitin, J. (2006). "The times they are a changing": Undertaking qualitative research in ambiguous, conflictual, and changing contexts. *The Qualitative Report, 11*, 209–228.
Kramer, R., & Lewicki, R. J. (2010). Repairing and enhancing trust: Approaches to reducing organizational trust deficits. *The Academy of Management Annals, 4*, 245–277.
Kvale, S. (2007). *Doing interviews*. London: Sage.
Labov, W. (1972). *Sociolinguistic patterns*. Philadelphia: Pennsylvania University Press.
Loh, J., Smith, J. R., & Restubog, S. L. D. (2010). The role of culture, workgroup membership, and organizational status on cooperation and trust: An experimental investigation. *Journal of Applied Social Psychology, 40*, 2947–2968.
Lønsmann, D. (2016). Negotiating positionality in ethnographic investigations of workplace settings: Student, consultant or confidante? In G. Alessi & G. Jacobs (Eds.), *The ins and outs of business and professional discourse research: Reflections on interacting with the workplace* (pp. 13–36). Basingstoke: Palgrave Macmillan.
Mishler, E. G. (1986). *Research interviewing: Context and narrative*. Cambridge, MA: Harvard University Press.
Morse, J. M., & Richard, L. (2002). *Read me first for a user's guide for qualitative research*. Thousand Oaks, CA: Sage.
O'Reilly, K. (2009). *Key concepts in ethnography*. London: Sage.
Peräkylä, A. (2005). Analyzing talk and text. In N. K. Denzin & Y. S. Lincoln (Eds.), *The Sage handbook of qualitative research* (3rd ed., pp. 869–886). Thousand Oaks, CA: Sage Publications Ltd.
Potter, J. (1996). Discourse analysis and constructionist approaches: Theoretical background. In J. T. E. Richardson (Ed.), *Handbook of qualitative research methods for psychology and social sciences* (pp. 125–140). Leicester: BPS Books.

Potter, J., & Hepburn, A. (2005). Qualitative interviews in psychology: Problems and possibilities. *Qualitative Research in Psychology, 2*, 281–307.
Richards, K. (2003). *Qualitative inquiry in TESOL*. London: Palgrave Macmillan.
Richards, K., Ross, S. J., & Seedhouse, P. (2012). *Research methods for applied language studies*. London: Routledge.
Sacks, H. (1992). *Lectures on conversation* (Vols. I and II). Oxford: Blackwell.
Sarangi, S. (2002). Discourse practitioners as a community of interprofessional practice: Some insights from health communication research. In C. Candlin (Ed.), *Research and practice in professional discourse* (pp. 99–135). Hong Kong: City University of Hong Kong Press.
Sarangi, S. (2007). The anatomy of interpretation: Coming to terms with the analyst's paradox in professional discourse studies. *Text & Talk, 27*, 567–584.
Sarangi, S., & C. Hall (1997). *Bringing off 'applied' research in inter-professional discourse studies*. Paper presented at the BAAL/CUP seminar on Urban Culture, Discourse and Ethnography. Thames Valley University, 24–25 March.
Schnurr, S., & Zayts, O. (2017). *Language and culture at work*. Oxon, New York: Routledge.
Silverman, D. (2001). *Interpreting qualitative data* (2nd ed.). London: Sage.
Speer, S. (2002). 'Natural' and 'contrived' data: A sustainable distinction? *Discourse Studies, 4*, 511–525.
Talmy, S. (2011). The interview as collaborative achievement: Interaction, identity, and ideology in a speech event. *Applied Linguistics, 32*, 25–42.

5

Measuring Competence for Global Business: In Search of Authentic Data in Japanese Business Corporations

Hiromasa Tanaka

Introduction

As players in business within the globalized economy, Japanese corporations implement language policies followed by training interventions to develop the global business competence of employees. While Japanese is the dominant business language in Japan's domestic markets, English is the most used language of business for Japanese business practitioners communicating globally. English communication is critical for Japanese business practitioners in dealing with potential and existing non-Japanese clients, partners, and in negotiating mergers and acquisitions of overseas companies. It is argued emphatically that developing highly communicative employees is key to globalizing organizations in Japan (Okabe 2018). Developing an awareness of English as a global business language is often a prime focus of language policies in Japanese business corporations. For

H. Tanaka (✉)
School of Humanities, Meisei University, Hino-City, Tokyo, Japan
e-mail: tanakahi@eleal.meisei-u.ac.jp

G. Jacobs, S. Decock (eds.), *Good Data in Business and Professional Discourse Research and Teaching*, Communicating in Professions and Organizations,
https://doi.org/10.1007/978-3-030-61757-8_5

example, in order to raise employees' awareness of the importance of English as a business language and also to develop employees' English competence, a number of Japanese business corporations implement English mandate policies which state that English must be the main corporate language (Takamori 2015). To this end, employees of Japanese business corporations receive training to gain (Business) English competence before being appointed to positions that require communication in English.

However, recent research has challenged the notion that English proficiency is the sole key indicator of job performance in intercultural business for two reasons. First, strong competence in English, as measured by standard English tests, is not always a reliable indicator of an employee's ability to perform well in business communication contexts (Ngah et al. 2011); rather, InterCultural Interaction Competency (ICIC) needs to be assessed (Spencer-Oatey and Franklin 2009). Second, ICIC tests currently available in the market are criticized for their cultural bias and their overgeneralization of competence ignoring locally specific contextual and environmental factors. Thus, a test for the Japanese context is critical if accurate insights are to be gained from this specific research site. Kubota (2013) elucidated these locally specific contextual and environmental factors in an investigation of interactions between Japanese expatriates and Chinese office workers who needed to use both written Chinese and Japanese despite the importance of English proficiency for oral interactions. The reason for this is that Chinese and Japanese languages use similar characters (*Hanzi* and *Kanji respectively*) and share several old Chinese proverbs because of historical exchanges between the countries. While the pronunciation of words and phrases is different, the written mode may support stronger communication in the absence of spoken comprehensibility. For example, when talking about feelings or beliefs, written communication could be clearer and more effective. English, however, might prove more effective in discussing mechanical or technological matters which involves knowledge from Western business society. The choice of which language to use for better understanding requires a deep appreciation of the historical context and sensitivity to the matters which Japanese expatriates encounter. Kubota (2013) argues that such translingual proficiency in business is supported by communicative and foundational dispositions, or characteristics, along with cultural knowledge. Several managerial procedures such as the decision-making process in Japanese business corporations have been developed under influences of historical, geographical and economic factors (Bargiela-Chiappini and Tanaka 2012). These systems are often divergent from those of non-Japanese business partners and sometimes confuse stakeholders. Therefore, a non-ethnocentric perspective would ensure Japanese systems and managerial procedures are understood by global business partners. If English-only is used, Japanese business practitioners are not able to successfully develop strong intercultural teams. Criticism of the linguistic and communicative competence of Japanese business practitioners may be miscalculated without considering the "contextual situatedness of linguistic competence" (Blommaert et al. 2005, p. 197). It is still unclear whether communicative and fundamental dispositions interact with linguistic competence; that is, to what extent linguistic competence is affected by inherent personal traits such as adaptability, cultural sensibility and resilience (Cumberland et al. 2016) and other situational variables including ways to develop trust and power relations (Yoshida et al. 2013). Studies on global leadership competencies in the field of Human Resource Development pinpoint fundamental dispositions or personal traits as important domains of competency. Cumberland et al. (2016) identify 17 personality traits consistently linked to effective global leadership. However, Holt and Seki (2012) argue that leadership models need to operate from a multi-cultural perspective involving situational variables. Findings from past business discourse research indicate that these situational variables have at least two factors. One factor is the shared history of Asian cultures; an example of this is the way Asians can convey, non-verbally, an understanding of others' religion, morality and trust (Bargiela-Chiappini and Tanaka 2012). Another factor is the locally situated environmental factor. For instance, vendor-client or sales-engineer relationships can differ depending on local politeness protocols or whether the interlocutors' organizations have 'perceived' technical superiority. The culturally acquired ability to 'sense' these factors could be part of Japanese specific competence.

It is primarily for these reasons that a more appropriate test of communicative competence in a intercultural context is in development. This article reports on one case of data collection and analyses to be used in scripting critical incident scenarios for the revised test. The term, Global Business Discourse Competence (GDBC) was coined to refer to ICIC and its capacity to represent specific discourse, in this case, the Japanese context. In order to understand such integrated competence, it is ideal to observe naturally occurring business interaction. However, in carrying out business discourse research in Japan, participating companies are concerned about protecting technical knowledge, employees' privacy as well as saving corporate face, making it challenging for researchers to access such naturally occurring business interactions. This paper reports on the process of presenting critical incident vignettes without access to naturally occurring interaction data. The vignettes were devised employing data collected from multiple sources and their authenticity was continually revised through review and dialogue with stakeholders until their authenticity was verified. Thus, the main question in this paper is whether business discourse data can be simulated authentically.

English Communication Competence in Intercultural Business Contexts

In order to further discuss Japanese business practitioners' communication competence in an intercultural context, it is imperative to trace the development of the notion of InterCultural Interaction Competence (ICIC), and address why attributing issues to 'culture' is problematic for ICIC research. Communication competence in intercultural business contexts has been approached from various perspectives across many different fields. Such competence is termed in numerous ways, including intercultural communication competence (Dai and Chen 2014), intercultural competence (Deardorff 2009) intercultural communicative competence (Planken et al. 2004) global leadership (Cumberland et al. 2016) and global management competencies (Bücker and Poutsma 2009). The competences (or competencies) discussed in these studies share some common elements even though each study emphasizes different aspects. Spencer-Oatey and Franklin (2009) use the term

"InterCultural Interaction Competence (ICIC)" as an umbrella term to refer to these competencies needed for the purpose of communicating appropriately and to handle dynamic outcomes that result from intercultural exchanges. First, I will conceptualise intercultural business communicative competence using the term ICIC, later expanding this notion to GDBC in the section on Global Business Discourse Competence for Japanese business practitioners.

In the context of past ICIC research, the language associated with intercultural interaction was often assumed to be English since it is the language of choice for intercultural communication. English competency is considered more important than any other language, particularly in Japan. English is the language used in the United States which has been the largest market for many Japanese business corporations since 1950's (Bargiela-Chiappini and Tanaka 2012). Furthermore, English has been the most frequently used business language, not only by Japanese, but also by Asian business practitioners since the end of the twentieth century (McArthur 2003). Thus, in ICIC research, the initial emphasis was placed on a high command of the four macro skills of English (reading, writing, speaking and listening) as the core required competence. These early studies emphasized competence in the productive skills of writing and speaking (Murphy et al. 1997), the receptive skill of reading which is required to improve writing style (Rivers 1979), and the skill of listening and paying attention to what others are saying (Goby and Lewis 2000). In Asia, corpus linguists provided a list of important English words and phrases for ICIC development (Chujo et al. 2007; Chen 2017). Later, the focus of ICIC research gradually shifted from linguistic competence to intercultural competence. ICIC studies in Asia also show this tendency. Du-Babcock and Tanaka (2013) argue that for business communication both linguistic and cultural competencies are critical. The most recent large-scale interdisciplinary study focusing on business professionals on mainland China is that by Yao (2019) who echoes Du-Babcock and Tanaka's conclusions that language and cultural abilities are both crucial to intercultural business communication competence. However, no studies have yet clarified what social or psychological elements are encapsulated in the term 'culture'.

The term ‘culture’, nevertheless, has been used to represent a range of concepts. Handford (forthcoming) cautions that the term ‘culture’ should be carefully treated in discussing business communication. According to Handford, culture can be defined in two ways, ‘culture-as-given’ and ‘culture-as-construct’, and he states that the two are mutually exclusive. Taking the former definition, culture is viewed as the concept of a fixed and predefined group that people belong to which predicts the actions, values, and interactional styles of the people in that same cultural group. In the latter definition, culture is seen as dynamic and heterogeneous rather than fixed and monolithic (Piller 2011). Fujio (2016), in her case study of a Canadian branch of a Japanese company, problematizes the term ‘culture’ by noting that it includes a wide range of concepts. In her study, Fujio analysed data from six interviewees (expatriates and local employees working in Canadian-based Japanese business corporations). She argues that differences on job sites are discussed using the phrase ‘cultural difference’, but that, in fact, some instances can be more precisely termed such as differences or variations in business protocols, organizational structure, and hiring practice. Furthermore, Fujio argues that people tend to attribute every difference to culture but purports that there are business and organizational factors that inform so-called ‘culture’ which implies a need to reconceptualize the term ‘culture’ to mean a social context influenced by managerial variables.

These critical reflections on the notion of ‘culture’ suggest that ICIC is complex and involves elements of linguistic, intercultural, organizational, and interpersonal communication. ICIC is highly context-sensitive as it is influenced by interpersonal (power) relationships, organizations, and (inter)cultural settings specific to particular situations and interactions (Spitzberg 2003). Researchers strive to identify those contextual factors. For example, Fujio (2016) identified nine contextual factors that affect communication. Handford and Matous (2011) emphasize the management of power relationships in their study of a construction site. In the following section, aligning with the theme of this volume, I review the data collection methods of past research in exploring factors of ICIC.

Data Collection in ICIC Research

Data collection in research related to ICIC varies according to the ontological basis the researcher adopts. A large body of intercultural communication research is based on a realist perspective and adopts a positivist approach. Large-scale surveys administered across the world are used to generalize truths about, for example, value orientation, which can explain people's actions (Trompenaars and Hampden-Turner 1997). This positivist approach enables researchers to identify and understand cultural patterns (Oetzel et al. 2016). Taking such an approach, Bachman and Palmer (1996) administered a large-scale survey to Thai learners asking about their use of strategic competence (part of ICIC). Although these self-report survey results are usually tested for validity and reliability, this data collection method still faces the possibility of participants faking their responses or making biased judgments in response to survey questions. The reason for 'faking' may, in part, be due to the fact that test takers might be concerned that their frank disclosure of their personal values may not be received positively by employers. Additionally, 'faking' may be prompted because participants know that companies use these surveys and tests for placement.

Qualitative data collection methods including interviews and ethnographic observation are often used by researchers (Davis and Henze 1998). From this perspective, ICIC is seen as a competency of meaning making through interaction. Researchers examine these meaning-making practices referring to the participants' beliefs and assumed notions (Peltokorpi and Clausenn 2011). Generalization of the findings is usually outside the scope of qualitative research leaving readers to draw conclusions by comparing the findings to their individual fields or workplaces.

Mixed methods of qualitative and quantitative data collection have been used in recent studies. Chen and Yang (2014) used interviews and surveys to explore cultural values, behaviours, perceptions, and strategies in an academic setting in the United States. Kankaaranta and Planken (2010) explored competences in intercultural communication in European multinational companies through an online survey and in-depth interviews. Yao (2019), in analyzing ICIC of Chinese professionals in domestic workplaces in China, mostly used questionnaires supplemented by interviews. All three studies combine the survey method with interviews. Although these self-reported data enable researchers to directly access the voices of those involved in an event, the data are typically based on memories, possibly reproduced or judged through the respondents' subjective views.

In order to reduce the risk of biased information being provided, researchers themselves need to personally observe and record what really happens at the actual worksites where ICIC is required. Such naturally occurring empirical meeting data are often used in language-focused studies. Handford (2010), for example, recorded numerous business meetings on sites where English is used, often interculturally. Poncini (2007) observed and recorded multicultural meetings. These studies also use mixed methods, statistical analysis of their recorded meeting conversation, and qualitative analysis of their observation data. For Handford and Poncini, the focus of their analyses was on language in use, such as word frequency, the use of personal pronouns, and the use of lexis. These detail-oriented studies of the use of language at real job sites indicate how people with high ICIC actually use language, but what is not discussed in these linguistic studies is the macro analysis of contextual factors involved in interactions which may ultimately influence ICIC. While ICIC factors have been explored qualitatively and quantitatively, measuring ICIC requires primarily a quantitative approach. The next section reviews current measurement methods.

Measuring ICIC

Several tests and inventories to measure or assess ICIC have been developed and some of them have been commercialized. Sometimes the word test and inventory are used interchangeably. The term "test" is generally used to refer to a device for quantifying competency while "inventory" is used to assess communication styles. Thus, test items require correct answers while for inventory items, all answers are accepted. Most are based on test takers' self-report or self-assessment. These devices usually use cultural styles or dimensions that have been developed in past survey-based research; for instance, Assessment of Intercultural Competence (AIC) uses Hofstede's cultural dimensions. ITIM Culture Management Consultants is also a self-report inventory where the participant reflects on a list of, for example, performance indicators, the result of which Hofstede (1984) used as the framework. Trompenaars and Hampden-Turner (1997) used seven dimensions of culture and corporate culture to give test takers each their own cultural profiles. In spite of the possibility of 'faking' discussed in the previous part, these tests and inventories are believed to provide "objective" feedback to test participants in terms of their styles and stance to deal with different culture(s). However, the chronological contexts that influence situated intercultural business interaction are not considered in these tests and inventories; neither are specific local environmental features of business interaction considered. Investigating regional differences in Japan in terms of intercultural sensitivity, Yamamoto's study (2014) suggests the need for the development of a way of measuring local contexts in Japan since Western perspectives of cultures used in the existing tests and inventories sometimes ignored local contexts. The roles of business practitioners, their general attitudes toward English and other foreign languages, management structures, and the values placed on specific aspects of business in Japan (and some other Asian countries) are, in fact, often seen as deviating from the general practice of Western business researchers and practitioners (Bird 2001).

Context of the Test Development Project

The present project was initiated and carried out by the Institute for International Business Communication (IIBC), an incorporated foundation in Japan. An IIBC market analysis of their institutional test users reports the users' strong demand for a test to measure ICIC specific to Japanese business practitioners. The large-scale research undertaken by Yao (2019) indicates that specific features of ICIC exist for domestic Chinese business practitioners. Therefore, it can be extrapolated that a set of specific features is also likely to exist for Japanese professionals. In order to emphasise the competence specific to Japanese professionals, the term GBDC is used in the project. Drawing on Gee's (2011) notion of Discourse with capital D, the word Discourse is chosen to refer to a socially constructed set of language and behaviour in a specific business situation. In view of an increasing need for Japanese employees to work in English speaking environments, Human Resource Development (HRD) managers of Japanese business corporations want tests that can predict their employees' performance in global business. These contexts include international alliances, joint ventures, consortia, sales and procurement of international supply chains, the management of merged or acquired non-Japanese organizations, and training and development of non-Japanese employees. Most business corporations refer to employees' scores of Standard Tests of English when appointing them to positions in which English communication is required. However, as HRD managers in Japan became aware that their employees' GBDC had to be assessed, the IIBC started to develop a new test in response to this increasing demand. A test development team was formed in 2015, consisting of researchers and staff from test marketing and research and development. I was asked to participate in the project. In this article I use the pronoun 'I' to mean the author as an individual researcher, and 'we' to refer to the whole test development team.

The review of past research poses the following question in the context of this test project:

> How can we identify GBDC factors from the obtainable data and validate them?

This article focuses on data collection and validation. While it would be usual to define the test constructs, meaning the concepts or characteristics the test is designed to examine, I am unable to disclose them for security and confidentiality agreements with the stakeholders. In the next section I will describe our data collection process and the authentication of the data.

Initial Data Collection and Analysis

Since there has been little research on ICIC for Japanese business professionals (GBDC), we needed to start from limited working hypotheses. To refine the hypotheses, we went through cyclical processes of data collection and analysis (Ulichny 1991). A development committee was formed which also included senior HRD directors from four multinational business corporations. This was because HRD departments are anticipated to be the largest market for this prospective GBDC test. In order to first develop hypotheses on the desired constructs of the test, six focus group meetings with the four corporate committee members were held in the fiscal year 2016 to 2017. After these focus group meetings, the test development team created and carried out an online survey (n = 300). This iterative process enabled the research team to build and test our hypotheses cyclically for a higher level of validation. In this initial data collection, we analysed factors that make high-achieving employees. These factors were further examined by subject matter specialists. Subject matter specialists removed factors that are job specific and less generalizable.

Our initial analysis resulted in the following hypotheses:

(1) HRD directors need to measure GBDC primarily for expatriates, and employees working in international alliances, partnerships, or consortia.
(2) GBDC have different or additional features compared to the competence factor list of existing ICIC research.
(3) Some selected ICIC factors from past research are useful in our analysis. It is important to use selected ICIC factors from past research.

At the end of this process, the test development team constructed 13 hypothetical factors which may relate to GBDC. These hypotheses, developed from the focus groups meetings and online survey, were subsequently used in the opening questions of in-depth interviews which were conducted to collect emic views from business practitioners recommended as high-achieving employees from the 21 participating companies.

In-Depth Interviews

In-depth interviews were carried out with 31 high-achieving employees from 21 business corporations. The test development team requested HRD directors of these business corporations to choose high-achieving employees. With the test development team members, I visited the offices of the companies located in Tokyo, Osaka, Ibaraki and Kanagawa prefectures. All the interviews were carried out in a room with recording equipment. I interviewed 21 employees and another team member conducted 10 interviews. A test development team member explained the confidentiality agreement which stated that the names of individual interviewees and the name of the organization would be anonymized and any data recorded in the interviews would be kept confidential unless the individual interviewee as well as the corporation agree to disclose them. The document was signed at the end of the interviews. The data consist of 46 hours of audio- and video-recorded interviews after which the data were transcribed (1 million Japanese characters) by professional transcribers. Each semi-structured interview lasted around 90 minutes. The interviews were conducted in Japanese in order to capture the interviewees' nuanced emotional expression. The interviews started with questions based on the hypothesized 13 GBDC factors. Then, the interviewers requested each interviewee to talk about problematic situations they encountered in their worksites and asked what kind of abilities were needed to solve the problems.

The interviewees talked about the difficulties in developing trustful relationships with host-country government officials and local employees, and the challenges in resolving issues that may have been caused by discrepancies between locals' and their employers' work values and ethics; these points resonated with the findings of past studies on Japanese business discourse (Okamoto 2008; Tanaka 2006; Handford forthcoming). In the interview data from expatriates who developed and led multicultural teams, interviewees repeatedly reported issues in management and leadership practices which impacted team building. Indeed, Du-Babcock and Tanaka's study (2017) on intercultural business meetings between Chinese and Japanese professionals showed the importance of strong management and leadership in team development and decision-making in multicultural interactions. As mentioned above in the Research Question, GBDC factors were also analysed using the interview data. These factors were examined by subject matter specialists. The subject matter specialists confirmed that the GBDC factors were a critical inclusion in global business situations. A factor analysis of the data from two pre-pilot tests (n = 276) found identical factors and the factors were reduced to a smaller number of test constructs. Although details regarding the constructs will be reported in another publication following the completion of the test project, in the following section some specific characteristics of GBDC will be explained.

Specific Features of Global Business Discourse Competence

The interview data indicate that Japanese high achieving employees know how to use particular ways of speaking and behaving, as well as strategies and supplementary communication resources, such as products or charts which are available in the specific situations in which they work. Furthermore, the analysis of iterative data revealed specific features of Discourse typical of intercultural communication, particularly for Japanese business practitioners.

(1) As mentioned previously, many interviewees came from the fields of investment, engineering, production, finance, and information technologies. There were few cases involving interactions with end-users or consumers.
(2) Most interviewees were native speakers of Japanese, and they used English as a foreign language. English was used as a Lingua Franca with non-native speakers and native speakers.
(3) The interviewees' actions were often influenced by an established business orientation strongly related to Japan-specific management and hiring practices.

(4) Interviewees' interactions often involved important people (mostly Japanese) whose command of English was typically at a less than satisfactory level.

The test development team takes an ontological stance and considers interactions on the job sites as Discourse. This Discourse (Gee 2011) adequately frames the data collected from multiple sources, including interviews, focus groups, and feedback from subject matter specialists. Business interactions are viewed as the process of creating meaning where language and action occur synchronously in specific contexts as mentioned in the earlier discussion of GBDC. Generally, Discourse encapsulates social interaction in given business contexts involving habitual actions, affect, social practices, and communication strategies (Bargiela-Chiappini et al. 2013). These Discourses are borne out of the unspoken and intrinsically understood conventions of the Japanese Human Resource Management (HRM) system and the Quality Control (QC) system, both of which have long-standing traditions. In the first case, the HRM system is built on an implicit employer-employee agreement where dedication is expected to be rewarded with job security. This means that a non-Japanese employee who is not aware of this 'tradition' might act differently to a Japanese who values this arrangement (Moriguchi 2014). In the instance of QC, many Japanese manufacturers operate globally and there is a tendency that when they expand their supply chains internationally and move their production sites overseas, they expect to also transfer their QC systems to the new sites. One such system is that of *Kaizen,* the Japanese philosophy of productivity which expects constant, continuous improvement and again dedication from employees. It requires production managers to communicate with workers about Kaizen or modify the system for workers who are unfamiliar with this Discourse which Aoki (2008) identifies as notable in Japanese domestic employment traditions. Thus, the goal of the test is to measure the extent to which GBDC enables Japanese business practitioners to perform these kinds of tasks in various cultural and social environments. GBDC is complex, involving not only the competence to communicate using linguistic, para-linguistic, and prosodic variables but also the competence to deal with situational factors such as conflicts raised due to power relationships, trust issues and technological differences. This is why we opted for a situational judgement test (SJT) to measure GBDC (Weekley and Ployhart 2006).

Situational Judgement Test

It is not easy to quantify GBDC, and yet, Human Resource Development Managers are required to present numerical data, typically test scores, to justify their decisions in hiring or placement practice. In an SJT, the situational or contextual description is limited, and the test-taker is restricted to choosing the 'best fit' response from the descriptors provided unlike in a 'self-reporting' method which is more open-ended and allows the respondent more room for constructing their 'ideal self'. In SJT, it is assumed that test takers will choose the option, from those available, that reflects how they anticipate they would ideally conduct themselves in real work environments. For this reason, SJTs are considered a more reliable predictor of job performance than self-report measurement because with less room for respondents to extrapolate, they are "less prone to faking" (Olau et al. 2019, p. 3).

Thus, for developing an SJT, the team needed to document critical incidents based on authentic events experienced by research participants and follow-up with questions to measure aspects being identified as important benchmarks in business competency measurement studies. To develop valid critical incidents, it was important to collect authentic first-hand data such as direct observations of human behavior on real work sites in which GBDC is required. Challenges included accessing such naturally occurring data because of Japanese business corporations' concerns about the potential for technical information leakage, with additional concerns around protecting corporate face. Furthermore, even with some companies consenting to us recording their employees on 'safe' job sites, the chances of capturing the precise moment of critical incidents were very limited. Our solution for overcoming these constraints was to utilize in-depth interview data mentioned earlier to create scenarios where GBDC factors are critical. We have replaced location, type of business, and where possible gender of the actors to protect interviewees' privacy.

Enhancing Authenticity of Critical Incidents

In order to reproduce authentic critical incidents in the intercultural business context (Flanagan 1954), we took an alternative approach to recording spontaneous data on job sites. We developed critical incidents from recurrent events in our data. In this process we referred to the vignette approach proposed by Tanaka (2006). Inspired by the notion of ethnographic 'realist tales' (van Maanen 1988), Tanaka devised a detailed vignette of a confidential steering committee meeting based on interview data from many of the meeting participants. The vignette was revised after receiving the meeting participants' feedback, in which research participants pin-pointed the parts that had been described differently from their real experiences. Also, some participants requested the removal of confidential data. The participants subsequently ratified the data. Tanaka proposed this vignette method as an alternative approach to reproducing inaccessible critical business interaction data by numerous revisions of vignettes based on participants' feedback whereby the authenticity of the vignettes is assured. At the same time the researcher can also protect the participants by eliminating private, confidential or sensitive information. This approach allows researchers to make "a situated and pragmatic ethical decision" (Richardson 2000, p. 932) about publishing the participants' private narratives. In a previous study (Tanaka 1999), I trialled the vignette approach and can report that some of the short movies have been viewed repeatedly (more than 80 times) by corporate managers in various countries, so once again I decided to use this method, this time producing 48 vignettes.

Data Analysis and Critical Incident Development Process

The critical incidents in which GBDC factors are required were created based on the contents of the in-depth interview data. The process of our critical incident production began with text mining of the in-depth interview data which identified recurrent semantic clusters. These clusters were codified using framing concepts developed in past ICIC studies (Deardorff 2009; Dai and Chen 2014; Du-Babcock and Tanaka 2017), and our analyses of the initial data. In order to assure the validity of the codified competence, four separate researcher analyses were undertaken and compared; from these, we selected and analyzed 22 competence factors, for example, distributed attention. Our research team then created 78 critical incidents. We reviewed the recurrent types of events in the interview data and reproduced incidents in authentic situations where problems typically arose because of the lack of the hypothesized competence factors. Furthermore, the vignettes were checked by peer debriefing of the researchers after which 11 subject matter experts (SMEs) from seven business corporations reviewed the incidents to verify authenticity. The experts checked for authenticity of business contexts, incidents, and actions within the incidents. Furthermore, two non-Japanese SMEs working with Japanese business practitioners in overseas subsidiaries of Japanese companies were interviewed to verify that non-Japanese participants also confirmed the authenticity of the critical incidents. In the next stage, the vignettes were video recorded with actors from similar cultural backgrounds to the business practitioners to maintain the authenticity of ELF business interactions. In order to assure a realistic rendering of the critical incidents, we carefully auditioned our performers. We selected actors with cultural backgrounds representative of the cultures in which Japanese business practitioners were likely to work in. We also chose actors with real business experience.

In order to provide a concrete image of the critical incidents, I will present an example script of a critical incident movie. Since the test development project in question is still in progress, confidentiality is critical. Thus, I use a vignette that I devised in an earlier research project. After my observation and interviews in multiple factories of Japanese manufacturers, I reconstructed this vignette from recurring episodes in the interviews. The incident was caused by participants' divergent views of training, and some usage of English expressions that were directly translated from Japanese expressions. Interview data indicated that differences between Japanese corporate training methods and a training method that a trainee might expect cause conflict. The data also indicate that although it is sometimes necessary to provide a careful and detailed explanation of the training principles to trainees from various cultural backgrounds, trainers generally take it for granted that their training methods will be understood by the trainee and sometimes do not explain principles adequately. One of the potential reasons for trainers' insufficient explanation is that communication in Japanese business can often be indirect and less verbatim in some situations (Fujio and Tanaka 2011). For example, Yokozawa et al. (2009) argue that in Japanese business communication, a kind of shorthand can be used because there is a shared background. Long-term employment in Japanese companies is the norm and turnover rate is much lower than that of other countries (The Japan Institute for Labour Policy and Training 2010). This is because people work together in the same company for extended periods and can understand each other with minimum communication. This could cause critical incidents as observed in the following scenario between a Japanese trainer and a non-Japanese trainee in a factory owned by a Japanese company and located in Japan.

Critical Incident

Situation: Miguel Perez was recently hired as an engineer by Sakura Electronics. The factory has been manufacturing computer fans since last year. Takeshi Ono is one of the Japanese trainers. Today he is working with Miguel Perez.

Ono: Look. This is the signal that indicates machine trouble.
Miguel: Oh. I didn't know what I should do.
Ono: Don't you remember what I did last time when I saw this lamp flashing?
Miguel: I don't even remember the lamp flashing.
Ono: Don't overlook anything I have done. The work in this area requires careful inspection of the products as well as the machine every 15 minutes.
Miguel: That wasn't in the manual I read.
Ono: No, it's not in the manual. It's our policy to do so. You'd better watch carefully. You are also responsible for the worker's safety.
Miguel: But Mr. Ono, it is impossible for me to pay attention to everything you do. I don't know what the most important things are to

learn. I think I need to understand more about the production system. I asked the personnel manager to let me attend a production management seminar, but my request was turned down.

Ono: When I started working in this factory, the senior engineers taught me very little. You know what I did?

Miguel: No. How did you learn Mr. Ono?

Ono: I watched the senior engineers very carefully. I tried to steal their skills and their knowledge. You have to learn the same way. Watch me carefully and assimilate my skills and knowledge.

Miguel: Mr. Ono, that's not my style.

Ono: Your style. Ha. I don't think you learn much from any style of training. You seem to have learned nothing since I came here to train you.

Miguel: Because you haven't taught me anything.

(Tanaka 1999)

The critical incident demonstrates the multi-causal nature of the issue. Influenced by traditional Japanese training methods and the typical education system, Japanese corporate training is somewhat different to that of non-Japanese organizations (McMurrer and Van Buren 1999; Bargiela-Chiappini and Tanaka 2012). The trainer and the trainee do not realize their differences. In addition, the underlined English expressions directly translated from Japanese expressions give the trainee the impression that the trainer is rather impolite. The serious face of the trainer also sends the trainee a negative message. The authenticity of this critical incident was reviewed by 84 training and development managers of 11 countries.

The example critical incident is about 1 minute and 49 seconds. The critical incidents in the tests are shorter. Each critical incident video clip was 30 to 50 seconds in length. Two SMEs monitored the filming process for the purpose of checking the authenticity of the interaction, setting, attire, and equipment. The team administered two pre-tests to further confirm the validity of the vignettes' content. In addition, the team interviewed participants prior to taking the test regardless of whether the vignettes were likely to take place on their job sites. The test development team believes that the interaction appearing in the critical incidents is close to reality. After test-takers view each critical incident, they are asked to choose the test item that best describes the issue raised in the first question, and the solution suggested in the second question.

Conclusion

At the end of this chapter, I revisit the question of whether the critical incidents based on second-hand data can be considered authentic. Scripting authentic critical incidents is indispensable in SJT for measuring GBDC because, for reasons explained in this paper, it was impossible for researchers to observe and record a variety of critical incidents as they took place on job sites. Researchers cannot predict when a critical incident will take place and on which job site. Gaining permission to collect data from business corporations was another challenge. Therefore, an alternative approach to collect naturally occurring data was necessary. Second-hand data, such as interviews, and focus-group meetings can be biased, but this chapter has demonstrated an example of using vignettes reconstructed from such second-hand data after the vignettes were tested for authenticity by repeat examinations and revision. In order to assimilate the vignettes to the reality of critical incidents influenced by contextual and social factors, the vignettes were acted out by professional actors, which I argue may have contributed to the authenticity of what is shown to test takers.

The critical incidents can also be used to effectively demonstrate issues on global business sites for trainees of GBDC training programs. The realistic critical incidents help trainees with little experience become aware of real-world business. While some might debate the efficacy of the critical incident creation approach proposed here in adequately representing authentic data, we believe it to be one of the best alternative methods of ethically presenting quasi-authentic data.

References

Aoki, K. (2008). Transferring Japanese kaizen activities to overseas plants in China. *International Journal of Operations & Production Management, 28*, 518–539.

Bachman, L. F., & Palmer, A. S. (1996). *Language testing in practice*. Oxford: Oxford University Press.

Bargiela-Chiappini, F., & Tanaka, H. (2012). Mutual gaze: Japan, the west, and management training. In S. Nair-Venugopal (Ed.), *The gaze of the west and framings of the east* (pp. 139–155). New York: Palgrave Macmillan.

Bargiela-Chiappini, F., Nickerson, C., & Planken, B. (2013). *Business Discourse*. London: Palgrave Macmillan.

Bird, A. (2001). *Encyclopedia of Japanese business and management*. London: Routledge.

Blommaert, J., Collins, J., & Slembrouck, S. (2005). Spaces of multilingualism. *Language & Communication, 25*, 197–216.

Bücker, J., & Poutsma, E. (2009). Global management competencies: A theoretical foundation. *Journal of Managerial Psychology, 25*, 829–844.

Chen, L. (2017). Corpus-aided business English collocation pedagogy: An empirical study in Chinese EFL learners. *English Language Teaching, 10*, 181–197.

Chen, J. J., & Yang, S. C. (2014). Fostering foreign language learning through technology-enhanced intercultural projects. *Language, Learning and Technology, 18*, 57–75.

Chujo, K., Oghigian, K., Nishigaki, C., Utiyama, M., & Nakamura, T. (2007). Creating e-learning material with statistically-extracted spoken & written business vocabulary from the British National Corpus. *Journal of the College of Industrial Technology Nihon University, 40*, 1–19.

Cumberland, D. M., Herd, A., Alagaraja, M., & Kerrick, S. (2016). Assessment and development of global leadership competencies in the workplace: A review of literature. *Advances in Developing Human Resources, 18*(3). https://doi.org/10.1177/1523422316645883.

Dai, X. M., & Chen, G. M. (2014). *Intercultural communication competence: Conceptualization and its development in cultural contexts and interactions*. Cambridge: Cambridge Scholar Publishing.

Davis, K. A., & Henze, R. C. (1998). Applying ethnographic perspectives to issues in cross-cultural pragmatics. *Journal of Pragmatics, 30*, 399–419.

Deardorff, D. K. (2009). *The SAGE handbook of intercultural competence*. Thousand Oaks, CA: SAGE.

Du-Babcock, B., & Tanaka, H. (2013). A comparison of the communication behaviors of Hong Kong Chinese and Japanese business professionals in intracultural and intercultural decision-making meetings. *Journal of Business and Technical Communication, 27*, 263–287.

Du-Babcock, B., & Tanaka, H. (2017). Leadership construction in intra-Asian English as lingua Franca decision-making meetings. *International Journal of Business Communication, 54*, 83–98.

Flanagan, J. C. (1954). The critical incident technique. *Psychological Bulletin, 51*, 327–358.

Fujio, M. (2016). The strength and weakness of Japanese globally minded leaders: A case study of Japanese manufacturer. *Journal of International Business Communication Association, 75*, 3–12.

Fujio, M., & Tanaka, H. (2011). 'Harmonious disagreement' in Japanese business discourse. In J. Aritz & R. Walker (Eds.), *Discourse perspectives on organizational communication* (pp. 81–100). Madison, NJ: Fairleigh Dickinson University Press.

Gee, J. P. (2011). *An introduction to discourse analysis: Theory and method*. 3rd edition. New York: Routledge

Goby, V. P., & Lewis, J. H. (2000). Using experiential learning theory and the Myers-Briggs type indicator in teaching business communication. *Business Communication Quarterly, 63*, 39–48.

Handford, M. (2010). *The language of business meetings*. Cambridge: Cambridge University Press.

Handford, M. (forthcoming). Training "international engineers" in Japan: Discourse, discourse and stereotypes. In L. Mullany (Ed.), *Language in the professions: Consultancy, advocacy, activism*. Basingstoke: Palgrave.

Handford, M., & Matous, P. (2011). Lexicogrammar in the international construction industry: A corpus-based case study of Japanese–Hong-Kongese on-site interactions in English. *English for Specific Purposes, 30*, 87–100.

Hofstede, G. (1984). *Culture's consequences: International differences in work-related values* (2nd ed.). London: SAGE.

Holt, K., & Seki, K. (2012). Global leadership: A developmental shift for everyone. *Industrial and Organizational Psychology, 5*, 196–215. https://doi.org/10.1111/j.1754_9434.2012.01431.x.

Kankaaranta, A., & Planken, B. (2010). BELF competence as business knowledge of internationally operating business professionals. *Journal of Business Communication, 47*, 380–407.
Kubota, R. (2013). Language is only a tool': Japanese expatriates working in China and implications for language teaching. *Multilingual Education, 3*, 1–20.
McArthur, T. (2003). English as an Asian language. *English Today, 19*, 19–22. https://doi.org/10.1017/S0266078403002049.
McMurrer, D. P., & Van Buren, M. E. (1999). *The Japanese training scene, Training & Development Magazine* (pp. 43–46). Alexandria, VA: The American Society for Training & Development (ASTD).
Moriguchi, C. (2014). Japanese style human resource management and its historical origin. *Japan Labor Review, 11*, 59–77.
Murphy, H. A., Hildebrandt, H. W., & Thomas, J. P. (1997). *Effective business communications*. New York: McGraw-Hill.
Ngah, E., Radzuan, N. R. M., Fauzi, W. J., & Abidin, N. A. Z. (2011). The need for competent work ready English language learners. *Social and Behavioral Sciences, 29*, 1490–1499.
Oetzel, J., Pant, S., & N. Rao (2016). *Methods for intercultural communication research subject: Critical/cultural studies*. Communication and Culture Online Publication.
Okabe, Y. (2018). Nippon Kigyou no Keiei Eigoka Senryaku: Rakuten no jirei wo chuusinni [Englishization of Management in Japanese business corporations: Case study of Rakuten]. *Kyoto Management Review, 32*, 207–220.
Okamoto, M. (2008). Examining the need for business communication competence in R & D departments: A case study of a pharmaceutical company. *The Journal of International Business Communication, 67*, 1–16.
Olau, G., Burrus, J., MacCann, C., Zaromb, F. M., Weihelm, O., & Robers, R. D. (2019). Situational judgment tests as a method for measuring personality: Development and validity evidence for a test of dependability. *PLoS One*, 1–19. https://doi.org/10.1371/journal.pone.0211884.
Peltokorpi, V., & Clausenn, L. (2011). Linguistic and cultural barriers to intercultural communication in foreign subsidiaries. *Asian Business and Management, 10*, 509–528.
Piller, I. (2011). *Intercultural communication: A critical introduction*. Edinburgh: Edinburgh University Press.
Planken, B., Van Hooft, A., & Hubert, K. (2004). Promoting intercultural communicative competence through foreign language courses. *Business Communication Quarterly, 67*, 308–315.

Poncini, G. (2007). *Discursive strategies in multicultural business meetings*. Bern: Peter Lang.

Richardson, L. (2000). Writing: A method of inquiry. In R. Kaplan (Ed.), *Oxford university handbook of applied linguistics* (pp. 923–948). Sydney: Oxford University Press.

Rivers, W. E. (1979). Lord Chesterfield on the craft of business writing: The relationship of reading and writing. *The Journal of Business Communication, 17*, 3–12.

Spencer-Oatey, H., & Franklin, P. (2009). *Intercultural interaction: A multidisciplinary approach to intercultural communication*. Basingstoke: Palgrave Macmillan.

Spitzberg, B. H. (2003). Methods of interpersonal skill assessment. In J. O. Greene & B. R. Burleson (Eds.), *Handbook of communication and social interaction skills* (Vol. 93, p. 134). Mahwah, NJ: Lawrence Erlbaum.

Takamori, M. (2015). Nikkei kigyo ni okeru eigo shanai koyogo ka no tejun to kanri taisei: Rakuten no jirei. *Doshisha Shogaku, 67*, 63–78.

Tanaka, H. (1999). Training and development. *Business World in English*, 26–29.

Tanaka, H. (2006). Emerging English-speaking business discourse in Japan. *Journal of Asian Pacific Communication, 16*, 25–50.

The Japan Institute for Labor Policy and Training. (2010). *Japanese working life profile: 2009/2010 labor statistics*. Tokyo, Japan: Japan institute for Labor Policy and Training.

Trompenaars, F., & Hampden-Turner, C. (1997). *Riding the waves of culture*. London: Nicholas Brealey International.

Ulichny, P. (1991). The role of hypothesis testing in qualitative research. *TESOL Quarterly, 25*, 200–202.

van Maanen, J. (1988). *Tales of the field: On writing ethnography*. Chicago, IL: University of Chicago Press.

Weekley, J. A., & Ployhart, R. E. (2006). *Situational judgment tests: Theory, measurement, and application*. Mahwah, NJ: Lawrence Erlbaum Associates Publishers.

Yamamoto, S. (2014). *A study of intercultural sensitivity in Japan: Embodiment and regional influences*. Paper presented at SIETAR USA 2014.

Yao, Y. (2019). *Intercultural communicative competence in China-based corporations: An analysis of Chinese professionals' perceived communicative needs, challenges, and strategies*. Doctoral dissertation. City University of Hong Kong.

Yokozawa, K., Steenhuis, H., & Bruijin, E. J. (2009). Recent experience with transferring Japanese management. *Journal of Strategic Management Studies, 2*, 1–16.

Yoshida, T., Yashiro, K., & Suzuki, Y. (2013). Intercultural communication skills: What Japanese businesses today need January. *International Journal of Intercultural Relations, 37*, 72–85.

6

Leveraging Student-Led Interviews in the Multilingual Workplace

Geert Jacobs and Astrid Vandendaele

For those interested in studying the role of language and communication in business and the professions, few settings can be more inspiring than the multilingual workplace. Whether we are looking at an international arts centre, a big multinational corporation with branches across the globe or an ambitious high-tech start-up, the series of relevant research questions is endless: which (foreign) languages are used for which purposes? What level of proficiency is expected? How are newcomers screened and trained? What are the costs and benefits of multilingualism? But also, from a theoretical and methodological point of view: how can we find an answer to these and many other questions? And, finally, zooming in even further, and chiming in with the overall issues that this book is concerned with, what kind of data can and/or should we get hold of in trying to answer these questions?

G. Jacobs (✉) • A. Vandendaele
Department of Linguistics, Ghent University, Ghent, Belgium
e-mail: geert.jacobs@ugent.be; astrid.vandendaele@ugent.be

G. Jacobs, S. Decock (eds.), *Good Data in Business and Professional Discourse Research and Teaching*, Communicating in Professions and Organizations,
https://doi.org/10.1007/978-3-030-61757-8_6

Following up on our earlier case-based explorations of the complex interactions between learning, research, and practice in the field of business and professional communication (Bruyer et al. 2016; Vandendaele et al. 2016), this chapter raises a number of questions on the use of collective data-gathering techniques as part of a wider, multi-site study on the multilingual workplace. Our dataset consists of the transcripts of the audio recordings of 65 semi-structured interviews conducted by graduate students of business communication in the organizations where they were about to start their traineeships (including corporate and non-profit settings and ranging from small start-ups to long-established multi-department companies). All 65 interviews focus on multilingual communicative practices in 65 different workplaces in Belgium, a country with three official languages, which allows us to gain substantial insight into the complexity of those practices. Through qualitative discursive analysis of the interview transcripts, we set out to identify a number of shared professional views on and practical applications of multilingualism. In particular, we will demonstrate how multilingualism is embraced as a strategic asset within the broader framework of glocalization and multinational marketing. In addition, whereas multilingualism is invariably encouraged 'on the shop floor' in an informal context, our findings show that there are formal policies regulating and restricting its use and that they vary greatly from organization to organization.

With a view to this volume's central question "What counts as data?" our analysis goes on to shed interesting new light on the affordances of collective data-gathering. Focusing on inter-interviewer variation, we take into account three recurring parameters (agency, lexical choices and formality) to identify three distinct interviewer personae in our dataset (viz. the Student, the Researcher and the Practitioner) as well as a number of complex patterns of role-switching and identity construction. We conclude the chapter by reflecting on the implications for the study of business and professional discourse and the roles of learners, scholars and practitioners in researching as well as providing training opportunities for the multilingual workplace and by presenting guidelines in order to strengthen interaction between these three sets of stakeholders.

Introduction

It is well-known that the scholarship on business and professional discourse research is richly interdisciplinary, attracting researchers in applied linguistics and discourse studies as well as communication sciences, sociology, management, marketing and studies of information systems. Even if we restrict our scope to the niche of what has been labelled "language in the workplace", there is still incredible diversity as Vine's 2018 *Handbook* demonstrates. In terms of methodology, for example, the academic efforts in business and professional discourse studies can be linked up with such wide-ranging scholarly frameworks as Critical Discourse Analysis (Mayr 2008), genre studies (from meetings, Bargiela-Chiappini and Harris 1997, to press releases, Jacobs 1999), Conversation Analysis (see for example Drew and Heritage 1992 for a pioneering work as well as, more recently, Antaki 2011), ethnography (Rampton et al. 2004), corpus linguistics (Handford 2017), linguistic pragmatics (Östman and Verschueren 2011) and politeness theory (Haugh and Watanabe 2017), to name but a few of the many paradigms that have proved inspirational in this area. There is an even longer list of topics that have been addressed, including humour, emotions, conflict, power, culture, gender, leadership and storytelling.

What distinguishes research on business and professional discourse perhaps most from other scholarly endeavours in the realm of language and communication is the very thin line between practice and learning; i.e. we notice how, in this specific academic context, the boundary between practitioners in a professional setting and students in the classroom is crossed more easily. In fact, the complex interaction between workplace research, practice and learning has started to develop into an important and exciting object of scholarly attention in its own right. Sarangi and Candlin (2010), for example, have discussed the impact of inviting practitioners to the classroom in order to share their expertise in a specific field of interest. More recently, Drury-Grogan and Russ (2013) have looked at how to integrate simulations of real cases in pedagogical settings. As Blake (1991) indicated early on, the ultimate step in bridging the gap between learning and practice is to get students out of the classroom and provide them with opportunities to work with practitioners in the field. This includes, but is definitely not restricted to, foreign language learning and issues of language proficiency (see Kerekes 2017). In exploring these subjects, we start to come to grips with the multifaceted role that language and communication are playing in helping learners transition into practitioners. In a previous study, we explored how students struggle to forge a sustainable partnership with practitioners and to translate their academic research in useful and practice-driven recommendations, and we called for follow-up studies to redefine both the students' and the teachers' roles in the collaboration (Vandendaele et al. 2016). Focusing on student research projects commissioned by external organisations, we argued that students should be encouraged to take on an ethnographer's perspective, with an increased awareness of their unique insider position as 'junior consultants' for the organisations (see also Bruyer et al. 2016 for an earlier investigation of the interfaces between learning, research and practice via the analysis of a student research project on Corporate Social Responsibility (CSR) in the pharmaceutical industry).

In this chapter, we combine an interest in one of the traditional topics of workplace studies, viz. multilingualism (see Lüdi 2017), with close attention to the intriguing space between workplace learning, research and practice as we set about experimenting with collective data-gathering techniques in which our students negotiate hybrid researcher-practitioner-learner identities. Our dataset consists of the transcripts of the audio recordings of 65 semi-structured interviews conducted by graduate students of business communication in the organizations where they were about to start their traineeships (including corporate and non-profit settings and ranging from small start-ups to long-established multi-department companies). The focus of the interviews is multilingual communicative practices in the workplace, but we also take advantage of the unusual setup to explore this volume's central question "What counts as data?", as well as reflect on the added benefits—and possible pitfalls—of this collective data-gathering technique.

Case and Data

The students who conducted the interviews under investigation were all enrolled in the master's program in Multilingual Business Communication (MBC) organized at Ghent University in Belgium. It is important to mention here that Belgium, a country with over 11 million inhabitants, is composed of three communities, each with a different language, i.e. French, Dutch and, to a lesser extent, German. The MBC students in our dataset are all Flemish, i.e. Dutch-speaking, with one exception: a French-speaking student from Brussels. Coming from diverse academic backgrounds—including economics, literature and linguistics, communication sciences, law and political science—the students make up a heterogeneous community, combining wide-ranging theoretical knowledge and expertise with different sets of methodological research tools. The one-year, 60-credit program helps them to acquire new practical skills as well as new theoretical knowledge in the field of business communication while also focusing on the 'multilingual' component with classes taught in English, French and Dutch.

One of the central principles underlying the program is a firm belief in the added value of the students' intensive interaction with practitioners. This takes many forms including simulation exercises, workshops led by communication professionals at their companies' premises, invited lectures by practitioners, a team-based research project commissioned by an outside organization and a 10-week traineeship at the end of the program. Each of these practice-driven assignments gives the students the opportunity to gain thorough hands-on experience with the challenges of business and professional communication in a real multilingual organizational setting. All of this has contributed to an interdisciplinary curriculum that aims to bridge the gap between learning and practice, to ease the transition from the university to the workplace. This is in line with the views of business communication students elsewhere in Europe as demonstrated by Aertsen et al. (2013), who argue that "one way out to address the expectations of both teaching staff and students is a teaching practice that helps students develop theoretically based practical skills" (322).

As for the 10-week internships in our program, we consider them both as a direct gateway to the professional world and as a unique research opportunity. The double role of the internship is encapsulated in the fact that we advocate it as fieldwork experience, allowing for a combination of (reflexive) ethnography and (hands-on, action-oriented) practice.

The 65 interviews that constitute our dataset in this study were conducted by our students in the organizations where they were about to start their traineeships. These initial interactions can be seen as a first contact, with the students getting to know some of the people they will be working with, but also as a starting point for their research, exploring what multilingual issues might be worth further scholarly scrutiny during their traineeships. The interview guide that the students were encouraged to use was structured as follows (Fig. 6.1).

Before the interview

Announce the overall focus on multilingualism and identify the main topics. Ask to conduct the interview in the interviewee's preferred language

At the start of the interview

Introduce the objectives of the interview in relation to the traineeship and the research project. Ask for permission to record.

Part 1 of the interview: the interviewee's background (5 to 10 min.)

Topics include: the interviewee's job description, professional experience, qualifications and training, and proficiency in foreign languages.

Part 2 of the interview: use of (foreign) languages in the organization (20 to 30 min.)

Topics include: the use of (foreign) languages for specific purposes, media and genres, and with different stakeholders; organizational language policies; developments over time; quality control; recruitment practices.

Part 3 of the interview: the interviewee's personal views on foreign languages in the organization (5 to 10 min.)

Fig. 6.1 Structure of the interview guide

In line with the requirements of semi-structured interviewing, the students were encouraged to ask broad, open-ended questions, go with the interviewee's flow and ask follow-up questions, encouraging the interviewees to provide illustrative anecdotes.

The resulting dataset comprises audio recordings and transcripts of 65 interviews, which lasted—on average—about 30 minutes. The interviewers were all graduate students of multilingual business communication who were enrolled in two consecutive years of the same one-year program and had completed all of the curriculum's regular courses. Each student was about to start the traineeship and end-of-year research project. The interviewees were all in a communication-related position at a wide range of mostly Belgian organizations, including government, NGOs, arts, non-profit organizations, communication agencies, and private companies. The latter ranged from newly founded start-ups to long-established multi-department companies, some local, others multinational. Most interviews were conducted in Dutch, yet three of them were held in English, in accordance with the interviewee's preference/nationality, or in case of an internship abroad. In this chapter, we present the interview extracts in the original language, with translations in English for the Dutch-language extracts.

Research Questions and Method

Based on the case and dataset identified in the previous section, we set out to address the following two highly open-ended research questions:

> **RQ1: What can we learn from our data about multilingualism in the workplace?**
>
> **RQ2: What can we learn about the process of data collection based on the interviews our students conducted at their internships?**

As for the first research question, through a qualitative content analysis of the interview transcripts, we set out to identify a number of dominant shared professional views on and practical applications of multilingualism. With a view to the second research question, we aim to contribute to this volume's focus on "What counts as data?" by looking at the affordances of collective data-gathering, e.g. does this technique have an effect on the quality of the data? Are there added benefits—or disadvantages—compared to single person data-gathering? In this part of our study, we rely on an analysis of (varying degrees of) agency, lexical patterns and register.

Findings

Multilingualism

Multilingualism as an Enriching Opportunity

Most if not all of the 65 interviewees in our dataset seem to embrace multilingualism as a very welcome condition that will have a positive impact on the organization. The active and widespread use of a range of different (foreign) languages, English and French in particular, is variously referred to as "an enriching opportunity", "added value", and "an asset".

> Extract 1[1]:
> *"omdat ik denk dat je niet alleen door de taal op zich en het vocabularium en de grammatica van de taal, maar ik denk ook dat de contacten die je kan krijgen met uhm mensen van andere nationaliteiten* ***verrijkend*** *zijn dus ik vind het sowieso los van dit bedrijf vind ik het een* ***grote meerwaarde zonder enige twijfel****."*
> "because I think that you do not just because of the language as such and the grammar of the language, but I also think that the contact you can have with uhm people from different nationalities can be **enriching,** so, in any

[1] All excerpts have been anonymized. All transcripts are available upon request.

case, apart from this company, I think it is a **substantial added value without a doubt**."

Extract 2:
"Eh dus ja, zeker een, ***een troef*** *en een* ***verrijking.****"*
"Uhm so yes, definitely **an asset and enriching**."

It is a predominantly positive appreciation that echoes the findings from Angouri's (2013) analysis of language policy and language practice in one consortium of three multinational companies as well as Grin's (2013) claim that the spread of foreign language proficiency across workplaces constitutes substantial macro-economic value. The optimism that dominates our dataset seems to contrast with a long-standing dissident belief in the study of multilingualism in the workplace about "Babel in business" and language as a barrier in, for example, HQ-subsidiary relationships (Harzing et al. 2011).

As far as our data are concerned, it needs to be pointed out that the fact that we see multilingualism being embraced does not seem to be in conflict with a deep-rooted respect for the local language. This observation is in line with Ehrenreich's (2010) study of the role of English and other languages as perceived by members of upper management in a family-owned German multinational corporation in the technology sector. In this study she shows that, in the twenty-first century, English has become an indispensable "must" in the company but that, despite the dominance of English, other languages are not disappearing from the scene and continue to be used as a pragmatic or strategic resource. The fact that multilingualism is a "must", is something we encountered often in our data. One of the reasons stated has to do with the official language requirements of the Belgian context (Extracts 3 and 4). Moreover, the growing need for English as a Business Lingua Franca (BELF) in an international context, is also flagged up in the interviews (cf. Extract 4).

Extract 3:
"Frans in tweede instantie, dat is als business partner ***een must****, back office wenselijk .... Ja, als je echt geen Frans kan, dan ga je volgens mij niet kunnen opstarten, omdat je altijd een telefoon in het Frans kan krijgen en als je dan niet de basisdienstverlening kan geven, dan is dat wel een issue. (...) Het is,*

> *momenteel, het speelt wel, als je het niet spreekt, ga je er volgens mij niet binnen geraken."*
> "French, in second place, that is **a must** for a business partner, highly recommended for back office … Yes, if you don't speak any French, you won't be able to start in my opinion, because there's always the possibility of receiving a phone call in French and if you are then unable to offer basic service, then that's an issue. (…) It is, at the moment, it is an issue, if you don't speak it, I don't think you will get in."
>
> Extract 4:
> *"De Nationale Loterij is een 100% overheidsinstelling, waardoor het Nederlands, Frans uh ja ne* ***must*** *is voor ons, en daarnaast zitten we in een internationale sport context dus is het Engels ook belangrijk. We kunnen bijna niet anders dan onze communicatie in 3 talen voeren."*
> "The National Lottery is 100% a governmental institution, which makes Dutch, French uhm yes **a must** for us, and, next to that, we are also part of an international sports context, so English is important as well. We are almost forced to communicate in 3 languages."

The seemingly effortless combination of local and particular concerns with more global, universal ambitions that speaks from our data can be seen to tie in with the broader frameworks of glocalization and micromarketing in a multinational business perspective (Robertson 1994). It is in sharp contrast with the overriding sentiments in other societal domains, education in particular, where multilingualism is considered by many as a problem or even as a threat (see Mortensen's 2014 study for a nuanced case-based view of how the pro-English language ideology that is so widespread in higher education translates into practice-based language policies that turn out to be very different). It should be noted in this respect that our data are exclusively related to white-collar settings: typically, the interviews that our students conducted are with managers or senior office staff and so they may gloss over some of the more critical views about multilingualism that exist elsewhere in the workplace, especially in blue-collar environments (e.g. Lønsmann 2014).

Although a lot of the people interviewed in our data set react positively to multilingualism, it goes beyond appreciation of the concept; a number of them seem to be purposely seeking it out, trying to launch strategic partnerships with new suppliers and customers who speak a different language. The following extract from one of the interviews illustrates this very well:

> Extract 5:
> *"Ja, eh, in principe, op dit moment werken hier een zes à acht mensen en die zijn allemaal Nederlandstalig maar, eh, wij werken wel, eh, een stukje bewust zelfs samen met, eh, anderstalige partners, leveranciers bedoel ik vooral, dat is vooral Frans, mensen uit het Brusselse, mensen uit Louvain-La-Neuve, en we hebben bewust ook voor hun gekozen om ons Frans hier een beetje op peil te houden, omdat wij op dit moment eigenlijk geen Franstalige klanten hebben, eh, maar wij, eh, wij willen die wel hebben, omdat ja, wij zijn een tweetalig land en als je nationale campagnes doet en wij hebben die in het verleden ook gedaan, dan willen wij met ons bureau, eh ja, ook wel nationale campagnes aankunnen. Dat is voor het Frans"*
> "Yes, uhm, in theory at the moment we have six to eight people working here and they are all Dutch-speaking but, uhm, we do work, uhm, deliberately in part with uhm foreign-language partners, I mean suppliers, especially French-speaking, people from around Brussels, from Louvain-la-Neuve, and we chose them deliberately to kind of maintain our level of French here, seeing we don't have any French-speaking customers, uhm, but we do want them, because, yes, we are a bilingual country and if you create national campaigns which we did in the past, that means that we uhm yes want to manage with our agency. When it comes to French."

Clearly, the interviewee in this extract indicates that it is important for his organization to position themselves as explicitly multilingual: it is an essential part of their corporate strategy.

Multilingualism, Gatekeeping and Skillification

For organizations that embrace multilingualism so unequivocally, it is not surprising to see that they insist on foreign language proficiency as one of the key gatekeeping criteria in selecting newcomers during the hiring process. The following extract is a fine illustration:

Extract 6:
"Ja. Eh, eigenlijk, wat dat voor ons nodig is, is dat we altijd werken met mensen die heel goed Engels kunnen en minstens één andere Europese taal. Dus eh, Frans of eh, Duits, of eh, whatever. Eh, en die, eh, toch al tien of vijftien jaar ervaring hebben in de HR-sector in een Europees land. Eh, plus misschien buitenland. Dus eh, ja, want altijd als wij een job post hebben, gaan we altijd, altijd is er een korte uitleg en dan is het altijd: mijn languages are English, French, Dutch, of English, German, of English, dat. Dus, allez, er is altijd een minimum vereiste van twee talen in de meeste bedrijven. Of soms drie. Dus ja, talen is ***echt wel een must.****"*
"Yes. Uhm, in fact, what we require, is we always work with people who speak English really well, and at least one other European language. So uhm French or uhm German or uhm whatever? Uhm, and people that, uhm have about ten to fifteen years of experience in HR in a European country. Uhm, plus maybe abroad. So uhm yes, because whenever we have a vacancy, we will always, there is always a brief job description, and it always states; my languages are English, French, Dutch, or English, German, or English, that, so, you know, there is always this minimum requirement of two languages in most companies. Or sometimes three. So yes, languages are **an absolute must**."

In this sense, our findings are in line with Peltokorpi and Vaara's (2014) work on so-called 'language-sensitive recruitment', which is identified as a key human resource management practice foregrounding foreign language competences and language use. They have demonstrated how taking a certain proficiency in one or more of the organization's foreign languages as a precondition for employment provides means for better communication and enhanced knowledge transfer, facilitates the development of international networks and makes it easier to bypass hierarchies.

Some of this has inspired a critical sociolinguistic perspective on the so-called 'commodification' of language. Heller (2010), for example, has written extensively about what she calls the "salience [of language] as a resource with exchange value" in the globalized new economy under the political economic conditions of late capitalism, in settings related to language teaching, translation, and performance art but also in tourism, marketing, and business communication (including, most prominently—iconically almost—, call centres). Related notions include skillification or skilling the self, as it was first presented in Allan's 2013 study of the key role of English in the communicability of immigrants as flexible labour, as well as language work (and the language worker); as for the latter, Thurlow's 2020 edited volume on "the business of words" makes a substantial contribution towards the 'high-end' wordsmithing practices of advertisers, public relations officers, dialect coaches and linguists whose talk and text gets "professionally designed, institutionally managed, and, inevitably, objectified for status and profit".

Regulating Multilingualism and the Belgian Situation

Whereas multilingualism is invariably encouraged in the office, 'on the shop floor', in an informal context, our findings show that there are formal policies regulating and restricting its use and they vary greatly from organization to organization. The dividing line seems to be between internal and external communication, where the former seems free and intuitive, and mistakes don't matter as much, whereas the latter is rigid, strict, and controlled. The following extract exemplifies the loose, pragmatic attitude towards the use of foreign languages inside the organization:

> Extract 7:
> *"Kijk mijn Frans, als je, als ik in het Frans een mail stuur naar onze Franse partner, tuurlijk gaan daar fouten in staan, eh. Het moet, eh, aanvaardbaar zijn en het moet begrijpbaar zijn, als je merkt dat het, eh, onbegrijpelijk is, dan moet je overschakelen, dan gaan we naar het Engels overschakelen."*
> "My French, you see, if you, if I send an email in French to our French-speaking partner, of course there will be mistakes, uhm. It should be, uhm, acceptable and it must be understandable, if you notice that it, uhm, is incomprehensible, then you should switch, then we will switch to English."

It echoes Angouri's (2013) analysis of language policy and language practice in one consortium of three multinational companies referred to above as it shows that the language policy in these multinationals is constructed as being flexible where both employees and managers typically take a 'what works' approach regarding language practice. Similarly Ehrenreich, in the 2010 study mentioned earlier, concluded when it came to English: "What needs to be learned, however, is not English as a native language but communicative effectiveness in English as a business lingua franca, which—as an international contact language—brings together non-native as well as native Englishes from various linguacultural backgrounds spoken with varying degrees of proficiency. Learning to cope with the challenges of such diversity, in the context of business communication, seems to happen most effectively in business "communities of practice" rather than in traditional English training".

In the Belgian multilingual workplace context, some of the linguistic choices are in fact determined by the government. "It's the law that determines the language we use", one of the interviewees comments, referring to the language legislation in Belgium.[2] Below, we can see this exemplified at the communications office of a governmental organization in Flanders:

> Extract 8:
> *"Ja in principe iedereen die hier een een openbare functie bekleedt of die direct contact heeft met de met de burger of mens die om om advies of wat dan ook komen vragen moeten altijd in het Nederlands te woord gestaan worden. Het gebeurt dat er mensen euhm op gesprek komen bij de schepen die het Nederlands niet machtig zijn en ik moet zeggen* ***alhoewel dat dat dan officieel niet mag*** *dan schakelen wij wel over allee of hij dan vooral maar naar het Frans is dat dan doorgaans"*
> "In theory, everyone who holds an official position or anyone who is in direct contact with the citizens, or a person who asks for advice or whatever, those people should always be addressed in Dutch. Once in a while, people uhm, who don't speak Dutch will visit the alderman and I have to admit that, **even though it is not allowed officially,** we will switch, or for the most part he will switch to, usually, French."

[2] According to Belgian language legislation, the language of official documents is determined by the linguistic region the company is in. Official (federal) documents should be written in the language spoken in that region. In Brussels, this means both French and Dutch. When it comes to various organizations, language policies have been decided on by the Flemish and the French Communities, each of them imploring organizations to communicate with staff in the language of the region.

Most often, there is a lot of freedom in the actual multilingual practices, and the comments concerning English and French in the abovementioned extracts seem typical of the Belgian context, in which almost all of the interviews in this study were situated. English is considered "the default language when dealing with foreign-language speakers", but French is considered "crucial". "As a Belgian company, you cannot afford to not be able to speak French", one interviewee argues.

Some even go one step further and argue that multilingualism is "quintessentially Belgian" and it is linked to the organization's corporate values.

Collective Data Gathering

In this second part of the analysis, we turn to what we can learn about the process of collective data-gathering based on the interviews that our students conducted at their internships. As we mentioned above, as a guideline for the 65 student-led interviews, conducted by 65 different interviewees, we introduced a list of questions. This was meant to help compensate for the inevitable differences that could be expected. However, in spite of our efforts to make the dataset as uniform as possible, we did notice striking individual differences. Drawing on an analysis of (varying degrees of) agency, lexical patterns and register, our main finding is that we observed a lot of diversity in the form of inter-interviewer variation. In what follows, we set out to demonstrate how we believe the diversity we encountered can be captured in the following three interviewer personae:

1. The interviewer as student
2. The interviewer as researcher
3. The interviewer as practitioner

The Interviewer as Student

A first group of interviewers approached the informants very much from a student perspective, drawing on a typical school assignment vocabulary, displaying a high degree of formality and positioning themselves as data miners who had low agency and aimed at closely following the predetermined script. The "interviewer as student" persona is perfectly exemplified in Extract 9 when, in the opening moves, the interviewer talks about preparing a "dissertation" and writing up a "research proposal". At least on two occasions he mentions that he "has to" do this. Overall, he uses tentative language and sounds uncertain with lots of hesitations and a number of modal auxiliaries, as well as highly formal, like when he asks permission to record the interview.

In the next extract from another interview led by a different student we see a similar level of tentativeness when it comes to exploring possible topics for the research project that the student is meant to conduct during his traineeship.

Extract 9:

- *IR: Wat ik juist misschien nog wou vragen, nu we het hierover gehad hebben, zijn er soms problemen of interessante invalshoeken die u ziet waarover u denkt van dat zou wel tof zijn als ik daarover zou schrijven? of ziet u niet direct…*
- *IE: Voor jouw thesis bedoel je?*
- *IR: Ja want het ding is wel, als het over die meertaligheid moeilijk is kan ik nog altijd een ander thema kiezen, maar in eerste instantie is het dus de bedoeling dat ik daarover (…) ik ga er sowieso zelf nog over nadenken maar het zou kunnen dat u zegt van dat is nu wel zo een probleem waarover misschien geschreven zou kunnen worden.*
- IR: What I just wanted to maybe ask, now we talked about; are there sometimes problems or interesting perspectives you see, of which you think that it might be cool if I were to write about? Or can't you think of anythinhg right now…
- IE: For your dissertation, you mean?
- IR: Yes, because the thing is, if it's difficult to do it about that multilingualism, I can always choose another theme, but to start off I am supposed to write about (…) Anyway, I am going to think about it myself but it might be possible that you say well, that is such a problem that might be written about.

Note as well how the student addresses the interviewee using the Dutch pronoun 'u', i.e. the formal version for 'you', indicating a perceived difference in status.

The Interviewer as Researcher

A second group of interviewers approached the informants from what can be seen as a researcher perspective, drawing on a scholarly vocabulary, displaying medium formality and a high degree of agency. The following is a good illustration:

Extract 10:

- *IR: Mijn thesis zal gaan over meertaligheid en nu ben ik nog op zoek naar een invalshoek vanuit [de organisatie]. Daarbij moet ik weten wat uw functie en verantwoordelijkheden zijn, maar dat heeft u al uitgelegd. Dus vroeg ik mij af wat eigenlijk het gebruik is van vreemde talen binnen [de organisatie]? Want bij mijn eerste gesprek met mevrouw xxx heb er al over gepraat en ze zei dat het moeilijk onderwerp zou zijn omdat [de organisatie] eigenlijk vooral Nederlandstalig is. Nu denk ik wel dat jullie toch hier en daar contact hebben met andere talen?*
- IR: My thesis will be about multilingualism and and at the moment I am looking for a perspective from (company). For that reason, I need to know what your job and responsibilities are, but you have already explained that. So, I was wondering what the use of foreign languages is like at (company)? Because, during my first talk with Mrs XXX discusses this and she said it would be a difficult subject because (company) is actually mainly Dutch-speaking. Now I do believe that you do get in contact with other languages here and there?

There is a lot more confidence on the student's part in this extract, with hardly any hesitations. Her take on the research angle is a lot more scholarly than that in the extract quoted earlier. When the student says she 'needs to' know what the interviewee's job and responsibilities are, the obligation seems to lie with her: she wants to know what the interviewee does because it can lead her to a good research angle, not because she has been told by her teacher to inquire into this—or at least that is what she argues.

Here's a second example, with the interviewer exploring various research options in collaboration with the interviewee:

Extract 11:

- *IR: Ja, maar inderdaad, ik kan dus ja met wat ik dit dit interview moet ik dan een soort van voorstel doen dat nog niet bindend is, maar van in welke richting ik zou willen verderwerken, dus ik denk dat wel iets nuttig kan zijn*

van die, ja, ***verschillende kanalen in crisiscommunicatie-setting, eh, hoe dat bedrijven dat dan doen****. Ik heb nog niet (…)*
• *IE: Hoe dat ze binnen één taal fluctueren dan*
• *IR: ja, ja*
• *IE: en en welke talen behouden blijven op basis van welke criteria*
• *IR: ja*
• *IE: eh, wordt er dan gekeken naar uw volgers, wordt er dan gekeken naar van wij zijn een internationaal bedrijf dus wij doen alles in het Engels*
• *IR:* ***Ja een andere focus zou misschien om het iets kleiner te houden****, bijvoorbeeld kijken hoe het in het Nederlands gebeurt en dan kijken hoe het in één andere taal gebeurt, bijvoorbeeld Frans of bijvoorbeeld Engels, en dan zien van (…)* ***Dan zal ik dat proberen verder uit te werken*** *eh, ja*
• IR: Yes, but indeed, I can so yes (…) based on this interview I have to come up with a kind of proposal that is not set in stone yet, but shows what direction I would like to go into, so I think it could be really interesting to, yes, about those **different channels in crisis communication setting uhm how companies then go about things.** I haven't yet (…)
• IE: How they fluctuate within one and the same language then
• IR: Yes yes
• IE: and and which languages are stuck to based on which criteria
• IR: Yes
• IE: will you be looking into followers, will you be looking at we're an international company so we do everything in English?
• IR: **Yes. A different focus might then be to keep it a little smaller,** for example how it is done in Dutch and to then look at how it happens in one other language, like for example French or English for example, and to then look at (…) **I would then try to further analyse that** uhm, yes

Note that in this extract the interviewer's repeated use of so-called continuers—for example, repetition of "yes"—encouraging the interviewee to carry on, is very much in line with the advice that is given to researchers on how to conduct semi-structured interviews.

The Interviewer as Practitioner

A third and final group of interviewers approached the informants from a practitioner perspective, drawing on a professional vocabulary, and displaying low formality and a high degree of agency. In the following extract, swift turn switches and a more or less equal distribution in the amount that each party is contributing to the conversation create the impression of a smooth interaction between colleagues and not of a student-practitioner interview.

Extract 12:

- *IE: Ik ben wel niet de eigenaar van [de organisatie] hé, dus ik weet niet euh*
- *IR: nee, dat is normaal niet erg … ja normaal is dat, alé geen probleem. Euhm … ja, het eerste deeltje gaat dus over uzelf, euhm, en dat gaat dus gewoon … wat is uw functie binnen de organisatie?*
- *IE: Euh showroom manager*
- *IR: Ja, en welke taken houdt dat dan precies in?*
- *IE: euhm dus showroom beheer, euh ontvangst van stylisten, euhm en verder ook, ja communicatie, euh de planning, euh naar klanten toe, euh Instagram onderhouden en, ja, allerhande taken*
- *IR: Ja, euh en daarvoor, welke achtergrond heb je zo qua opleiding en jobs die je—*
- *IE: Communicatiewetenschappen*
- *IR: Ahja. En dat is uw eerste job hier? Of heb je daarvoor-*
- *IE: Euh neen. Ik heb al euhm in een architectenbureau gewerkt voor de communicatie te onderhouden, en daarnaast heb ik ook al voor iemand gewerkt die euh magazines maakte, euhm en nog voor een journalist heb ik ook al gewerkt.*
- IE: I am not the owner of [company), you know, so I don't know uhm
- IR: No, that should not matter normally … yes, normally that is, you know, not a problem. Uhm … yes, the first little part is about you, uhm, and that is just about … what is your job within the organization?
- IE: Uhm showroom manager
- IR: Yes, and which tasks does that comprise?
- IE: uhm so showroom management, uhm hosting stylists, uhm and furthermore also yes communication, uhm, planning, uhm towards customers, uhm updating Instagram, and yes various tasks
- IR: Yes, uhm, and before that, what is your background, when it comes to education and jobs you
- IE: Communication sciences
- IR: Oh right. And that is your first job here? Or did you before
- IE: Uhm no. I have already uhm worked at an architecture agency maintaining communication, and next to that I have also worked for someone who made uhm magazines, uhm and also for a journalist I have worked as well

The following is perhaps even clearer. Here the student sounds very informal indeed, with the use of the direct, informal second person address ("vindt ge" instead of "u"), of substandard forms ("da" instead of "dat") and of a more relaxed vocabulary that deviates substantially from the script that the student had been provided with (e.g. the use of 'strubbelingen').

Extract 13:

- IR: *Ik ga misschien nog vlug efkes overgaan naar het persoonlijke deel, want ik denk dat we al redelijk goeie antwoorden daarop hebben. Uw persoonlijk visie op vreemde talen in organisaties, vindt ge da leuk, persoonlijk, om Engels te praten hier als die, eh, Spaanse Erasmusstudent hier is? Vindt ge da verrijkend ook voor iedereen of ziet ge dat eerder, misschien, als een bedreiging, niet persoonlijk voor u dan, maar voor andere mensen die misschien niet iets minder Engels kunnen? Denkt ge dat daar wat strubbelingen kunnen door ontstaan of niet?*
- IR: Maybe I'll just quickly go to the personal part, 'cause I think we have a few really good answers there. Y'r personal take on foreign languages in organizations, d'ya like that, personally, to speak English here if that uhm Spanish Erasmus-student is here? D'ya think it's enriching also for all of you or d'ya see it more, maybe, as a threat, not to ya personally that is, but to other people who maybe speak a little less English? D'ya think that problems may arise because of that or not?

It should be noted that the three personae sketched above do not constitute fixed and clearly delineated categories. On the contrary, we believe that there is a continuum of identity construction with some students in the same category identifying to a greater or lesser extent with a particular persona than others. In some cases, there is even an evolution in the course of the 30-minute interview with some interviewers starting out very much as students and gradually embracing a researcher or practitioner persona; it would be interesting to look at what role the interviewer plays in this.

What is perhaps most striking about our findings is that they seem to correspond with what came out of our previous work on how to bridge the classroom and real-world practice in the area of business and professional communication (Vandendaele et al. 2016). Based on our analysis of the interactions between students, academic staff and professionals in the context of student research projects commissioned by external organizations, we pointed to the challenges involved in bringing together the worlds of learning, scholarship and practice. It is exactly these three worlds that are represented in the different personae we presented above. The present analysis has also demonstrated that it is the same two parameters, viz. freedom and mutuality, that seem to distinguish them, with the researcher persona showing more freedom (e.g. vis-à-vis the script to be followed) than the student persona and the practitioner persona showing more mutuality (e.g. partnering up with the interviewee).

Conclusions

It is time to return to this volume's central question and reflect on what we can learn from the case presented here as to what counts as data in the study of business and professional discourse.

Clearly, our collective data-gathering efforts by means of student-led interviews have generated substantial diversity, with the students slipping into different personae as they go about their interviewing assignment. It is simply unrealistic to expect that each interviewer will be presenting each question in exactly the same way to each interviewee. And even if it was not, there would be no way in which we could expect the interviewees to co-construct the interviews in exactly the same fashion (cf. Briggs's *Learning how to ask* (1984). We believe that, as researchers, we need to be aware of this so-called 'inter-interviewer variation' and that, if we are, we can actually embrace it as an "asset". In our view, genuine awareness of this diversity implies taking the contextualization of our research efforts very seriously: in proceeding towards the analytical stage, we need to recognize that the interviews are deeply embedded in the program's traineeship efforts and to acknowledge the power dimension involved in this. This includes mapping how students behave in the process of negotiating access, gaining trust and constructing a professional identity for themselves (one that may or may not be in conflict with their role as students/researchers).

Crucially, it can be argued that all of this does not just apply to the collective data-gathering efforts by means of student-led interviews that we have pursued in the research reported here; it applies to the study of business and professional discourse in general. Variation and diversity are intrinsic features of most data that can be gathered in this field, whether we involve our students or not. And coming to grips with the essential contextedness of all business and professional discourse is a key requirement, no matter if we explore issues of multilingualism in Belgian organizations or something completely different. Any data, including audio and video recordings, interview transcripts or the results of survey research, are deeply and unavoidably embedded in the organisational context where they originate, and they are bound to entail profound power asymmetries that impact on what people say or write. It follows that standardized data (where data are perfectly comparable across settings) is not just a myth in business and professional discourse studies; it is not even desirable. Instead, the intrinsic diversity of the discursive repertoire constitutes a rich basis for analysis in its own right.

All of this points to at least one implication for how students, scholars and practitioners can work together in researching the multilingual workplace, one that can be taken to serve as a guideline in order to strengthen interaction between them: we should try to make our students aware of the different personae they may be slipping into as they gather (interview) data for the study of business and professional discourse. This could include analysing interview transcripts together, something that will help them on the exciting path from learning to practice that we have described elsewhere before.

Let us end this chapter by circling back, once more, to the question "What counts as data?" in the study of business and professional discourse, in general, and to one of the key notions spelled out in the introduction to this volume, viz. that of background and the question how familiar we need to be, as analysts, with the data that we are studying. In the context of our case study, the latter ties in with that other key notion authenticity: since the data gathering was subcontracted to the students, it could be argued that the data discussed in this study are—from the analysts' point of view at least—second-hand, hence not 100 percent authentic as there is a gap between the researchers and the practitioners that prevents us from reaching a deep understanding of what is going on in the interviews. While we believe these reservations make sense, we would like to argue that they call for a more comprehensive discussion on how researchers can collaborate and share results, and on how researcher positioning is affected. These questions are especially pertinent when it comes to the complex interactions between scholars, learners and practitioners, where—we have seen—identities are fluid and boundaries get blurred: as students put on researchers' hats while proceeding on the path towards practice, no one's perspective on the data can simply be taken for granted and the scholar-researcher-practitioner arena becomes an object worthy of study in its own right.

References

Aertsen, T., Jaspaert, K., & Van Gorp, B. (2013). From theory to practice: A crisis simulation exercise. *Business Communication Quarterly, 76*, 322–338.

Allan, K. (2013). Skilling the self: The communicability of immigrants as flexible labour. In e. A. Duchêne, M. Moyer, & C. Roberts (Eds.), *Language, migration and social (in)equality: A critical sociolinguistic perspective on institutions and work* (pp. 56–78). Bristol: Multilingual Matters.

Angouri, J. (2013). The multilingual reality of the multinational workplace: Language policy and language use. *Journal of Multilingual and Multicultural Development, 34*, 564–581.

Antaki, C. (2011). *Applied conversation analysis: Intervention and change in institutional talk*. New York: Springer.

Bargiela-Chiappini, F., & Harris, R. (1997). *The languages of business: An international perspective*. Edinburgh: Edinburgh University Press.

Blake, B. L. (1991). Student research in the classroom: Solving the teacher/researcher dilemma. *Business Communication Quarterly, 54*, 73–75.

Briggs, C. (1984). Learning how to ask: Native Metacommunicative competence and the incompetence of fieldworkers. *Language in Society, 13*, 1–28.

Bruyer, T., Jacobs, G., & Vandendaele, A. (2016). Good pharma? How business communication research can help bridge the gap between students and practitioners. *Business and Professional Communication Quarterly, 79*, 141–153.

Drew, P., & Heritage, J. (1992). Analyzing talk at work: An introduction. In P. Drew & J. Heritage (Eds.), *Talk at work. Interaction in institutional settings* (pp. 3–65). Cambridge: Cambridge University Press.

Drury-Grogan, M. L., & Russ, T. L. (2013). A contemporary simulation infused in the business communication curriculum: A case study. *Business Communication Quarterly, 76*, 304–321.

Ehrenreich, S. (2010). English as a business lingua Franca in a German multinational corporation: Meeting the challenge. *Journal of Business Communication, 47*, 408–431.

Grin, F. (2013). Language policy, ideology and attitudes: Key issues in Western Europe. In R. Bayley, R. Cameron, & C. Lucas (Eds.), *The Oxford handbook of sociolinguistics* (pp. 629–650). Oxford: Oxford University Press.

Handford, M. (2017). Corpus linguistics. In B. Vine (Ed.), *The Routledge handbook of language in the workplace*. Abingdon: Routledge.

Harzing, A.-W., Köster, K., & Magner, U. (2011). Babel in business: The language barrier and its solutions in the HQ-subsidiary relationship. *Journal of World Business, 46*, 279–287.

Haugh, M., & Watanabe, Y. (2017). (Im)politeness theory. In B. Vine (Ed.), *The Routledge handbook of language in the workplace* (pp. 65–76). New York: Routledge.

Heller, M. (2010). The commodification of language. *Annual Review of Anthropology, 39*, 101–114.

Jacobs, G. (1999). *Preformulating the news: An analysis of the metapragmatics of press releases*. Amsterdam/Piladelphia: John Benjamins Publishing.

Kerekes, J. (2017). Language preparation for internationally educated professionals. In B. Vine (Ed.), *The Routledge handbook of language in the workplace* (pp. 413–424). New York: Routledge.

Lønsmann, D. (2014). Linguistic diversity in the international workplace: Language ideologies and processes of exclusion. *Multilingua—Journal of Cross-Cultural and Interlanguage Communication, 33*, 89–116.

Lüdi, G. (2017). Identity in the workplace in a context of increasing multilingualism. In B. Vine (Ed.), *The Routledge handbook of language in the workplace* (pp. 348–360). New York: Routledge.

Mayr, A. (2008). *Language and power: An introduction to institutional discourse*. A&C Black.

Mortensen, J. (2014). Language policy from below: Language choice in student project groups in a multilingual university setting. *Journal of Multilingual & Multicultural Development, 35*, 425–442.

Östman, J. O., & Verschueren, J. (Eds.). (2011). *Pragmatics in practice* (Vol. 9). Amsterdam/Philadelphia: John Benjamins Publishing.

Peltokorpi, V., & Vaara, E. (2014). Knowledge transfer in multinational corporations: Productive and counterproductive effects of language-sensitive recruitment. *Journal of International Business Studies, 45*, 600–622.
Rampton, B., Tusting, K., Maybin, J., Barwell, R., Creese, A., & Lytra, V. (2004, December). UK linguistic ethnography: A discussion paper. In *UK Linguistic ethnography forum* (pp. 1–24).
Robertson, R. (1994). Globalization or glocalization? *Journal of International Communication, 1*, 33–52.
Sarangi, S., & Candlin, C. N. (2010). Applied linguistics and professional practice: Mapping a future agenda. *Journal of Applied linguistics and professional practice, 7*, 1–9.
Thurlow, C. (2020). *The business of words*. London: Routledge.
Vandendaele, A., Bruyer, T., & Jacobs, G. (2016). We never even wondered whether we trusted them or not: From freedom to mutuality in a student research project. In G. M. Alessi & G. Jacobs (Eds.), *The ins and outs of business and professional discourse research : Reflections on interacting with the workplace* (pp. 102–116). London: Palgrave Macmillan.

7

Coworking: A Rhetorical Enterprise Situated in Place

Deborah C. Andrews

Introduction

Broad advances in technology have opened opportunities for entrepreneurs to rethink and, in current terms, disrupt, long established and institutionalized sectors of the economy. Airbnb, for example, has disrupted the hotel industry. Lyft and Uber have disrupted the transportation industry, both taxis and rental cars. In doing so, they have also contributed to—and built their platforms on—what has come to be called the "sharing economy": home-owners sharing vacant rooms or second homes; car owners, not professional drivers, sharing time in their cars. To this list of economic sectors poised for disruption add the office. Mobile information and communication technology (ICT), among other forces, has led to changes in the concept of work and decoupled work and workers from the fixed office spaces of existing corporations. "Mobility and

D. C. Andrews (✉)
University of Delaware, Newark, DE, USA
e-mail: dandrews@udel.edu

G. Jacobs, S. Decock (eds.), *Good Data in Business and Professional Discourse Research and Teaching*, Communicating in Professions and Organizations,
https://doi.org/10.1007/978-3-030-61757-8_7

ubiquitous technological connectivity of work mean that the office is no longer a stable entity in terms of place, as office work can be carried out in multiple kinds of spaces" (Laing and Bacevice 2013, p. 39).

This new concept of work, largely aimed at creating new knowledge and driving innovation, and a new choice in location of work have inspired entrepreneurs to create a new kind of commercial workplace. These are coworking enterprises, part office with advanced technology and part social setting, available for short- or longer-term rental. A researcher at the Harvard Business School argues, "We have not reinvented office space in 50 years, so WeWork [the original corporate disruptor] is moving into white space" (quoted in WeWork's IPO: Risky Business 2019).

In emerging from the sharing economy, these new workspaces also reflect a widening assumption that collaboration, especially across disciplines, cultures, and perspectives, is the key to knowledge work. Collaborative communicative practices are essential to solve messy problems and pursue new opportunities in the twenty-first Century global economy. In my larger research project, I've been addressing how, or whether, a physical environment, like a coworking space, can be designed explicitly to foster collaborative communication (Andrews 2016, 2017, 2018). As newly designed places for a new kind of work, coworking spaces provided an appealing research opportunity.

The invitation to contribute to this volume inspired me to look more closely at a source of data that I'd seen simply as background reading for that project: the marketing pitches, the stories about coworking, that founders of such spaces deliver on their websites. To do so, I'm taking something of a detour from my larger project, which aims to disrupt communications research by focusing less on what is said and done in a workplace and more on the agency of place itself in that activity. The research presented in this chapter is less about the actual agency of place than about how the language in these marketing pitches, considered as both text and images, creates a spatial experience. Coworking spaces are arguably rhetorical enterprises situated in place.

To address this argument, I first discuss my data and research method in terms of this volume's central themes: authenticity, triangulation through a mix-methods approach, saturation, and background. Because these pitches represent real places, the section on background reviews the development of coworking spaces as I've researched their growth in relationship to communicative practices. That review of enterprises on the ground sets the context for this study of their recreation as rhetorical enterprises online. The main section of the chapter details the rhetorical strategies used to create the stories of coworking in five websites that are the focus of my study. The conclusion reiterates major findings and suggests topics for future research.

Two Limitations

One limitation to the description of my research data in this chapter is its presentation in print. These pitches, in full color online, are highly visual. They incorporate videos and music. Text and images *move*. The background section in this chapter includes photographs of a coworking space as a way to at least suggest what such spaces look like.

As I write in Spring 2020, however, the major limitation to coworking as a subject of study and, more significant, as an enterprise, is the general global economic collapse in response to the Covid-19 virus pandemic. Lock-down orders intended to prevent the spread of the virus have forced companies and other institutions to close and required workers to work from home. Under these circumstances, social distancing, as it has come to be called, has overridden the chief value promoted by coworking, that is, face-to-face social engagement and a sense of community. Many coworking spaces have also closed, and their reopening is uncertain. But the research remains pertinent for the time researched, conditions that may return after the pandemic subsides. Addresses for the websites in my study appear with the references and were valid in early 2020. Publicly available, the sites would be worth a visit as a companion activity to reading this chapter.

The Culture of Coworking

Even before Covid-19, WeWork, once the largest manager of coworking spaces in the world, was in serious financial trouble. Indeed, in his 2015 review of literature on coworking, Gandini (2015) argues that empirical findings about whether coworking can achieve its promise are few. He focuses on what he characterizes as the inevitably positive picture provided by academics and practitioners of such enterprises. The concept, he insists, may simply reflect an "illusory enthusiasm" used for "branding, marketing and business purposes" (202–203). For the study discussed in this chapter, however, it's the creation of that illusion that matters and is the center of my analysis.

A ground-breaking 2013 collection, *The Style of Coworking: Contemporary Shared Workspaces* by Davies and Tollervey, set me on course for this study. It includes statements by founders of 30 "hot" coworking spaces worldwide as well as abundant images of each. What the founders said was not reliable evidence for what was actually happening in their spaces. But in themselves, and with their emphasis on style, the statements seemed to cultivate an intriguing image of a culture of coworking. To follow up on their stories, I searched online for the websites of these 30 spaces in 2019. Some enterprises had disappeared or morphed into event spaces or restaurants. But many had continued and were thriving, demonstrating their staying power in the growing but fragile shared workplace industry. The arguments on their websites were deeply layered and, I thought, could sustain serious analysis, especially looked at through a mixed approach incorporating my research in material culture studies, in design, and in rhetorical theory.

Davies and Tollervey (2013) see coworking as having "its own unique aesthetic and *form of expression*" (7, italics added). Mostly as a critic, Gandini (2015) discusses the "'celebratory framework' that surrounds the *representations* of proliferating coworking spaces" (193, italics added). Such statements about expression and representations further validated for me my instinct that the pitches were worth attention. They helped me turn something previously taken for granted as simply part of a literature review into the data base.

Authenticity

Business and professional discourse occurs, by definition, in the context of work and the workplace. The physical environment of an office, however configured, or another place of work shapes, reflects, and sometimes subverts the kind of communication required to get work done there. That's the hypothesis of my larger project. To inform myself about communication at work, I've visited a range of workplaces, including coworking spaces; talked both formally and informally with practitioners; and read extensively not only in the academic and but also in the commercial literature of workplace design.

For this study, I've put aside questions about the agency of place in the real world. Instead, I'm looking at what might be considered the agency of text and images to create a virtual workplace that represents the real one. In the five sites in my research that agency has depended in part on the crafting of a rhetorical persona, someone of good character, presumably the founder-entrepreneur, who speaks for the space. The persona is an artifice, not authentic in any standard sense. It sets the frame for the fabrication of the larger artifice, a persuasive story about coworking.

Triangulation

In triangulating on how these representations, these stories, were put together, I incorporated methods from material culture studies, which looks at the effect of place on people's behavior and experience in the place, and design thinking, which creates places to achieve the desired behavior. In addition, beyond these methods, which I foreground in my larger study, I relied on theory and methods in classical rhetoric, something I'd taught for years. Rhetoric became dominant, the primary driver for choosing and analyzing the data. The following section briefly describes my mixed-methods approach.

Researchers in material culture studies examine the relationship between people and their things. This is in itself an interdisciplinary field that grew out of anthropology, art, history, and sociology, among other disciplines. Citing Pierre Bourdieu, anthropologist Danny Miller (2010,

p. 23), for example, notes, "Things, not mind you, individual things, but the system of things, with their internal order, make us the people we are". "In short, objects create subjects much more than the other way around" (Miller 2008, p. 287). From that perspective, a place, like a workplace, is inherently social and invites investigations into how people shape and are shaped by it. It is defined by its use, by the relationship among its inhabitants, by behavior there and its cultural norms. It is in flux. Place motivates certain specific actions, unlike space, which is experienced similarly by everyone and provides the opportunity for action (Overmyer and Carlson 2019). Without probably being aware of it, the spokespersons on these websites build their argument on the assumption that the place they have created can foster the kinds of behavior their customers seek.

A second method, drawing in some respects on material culture studies, is design thinking. Developed by architects, interior designers, and engineers, it is a process put into practice by international office design firms like Gensler and manufacturers of office furniture like Herman Miller. As David Kelley, a co-founder of the international space design consultancy IDEO argues, space should be thought of not as something "fixed-as-given, a facilities project or a showcase." It should instead be considered an "instrument for innovation and collaboration.... A valuable tool that can help you create deep and meaningful collaborations in your work and life" (quoted in Doorley and Witthoft 2012, p. 5). Aesthetic concerns have marked coworking spaces from their roots as an artsy underground movement to the high style enterprises today, so attention to design features is critical in the pitches, and in analyzing the pitches.

Third, and enveloping the other two approaches, is theory, along with method, derived from classical rhetoric. The art of persuasion is ancient, but it is easily refreshed to provide strategies for representing these new work environments. Because of its central importance, my rhetorical method is detailed later in the chapter.

Saturation

This study is not intended to be a thorough investigation of all coworking space websites, or even all those in a particular region, or of whether the claims in these sites are true. In particular, I put aside any validation of the websites' claims. I chose instead to take the sites' founders at their word and to be suggestive in my analysis, based on a small sample of five sites emerging from those featured in Davies and Tollervey (2013). They represent different regions internationally (and explicitly not in the US, for diversity); different demographics, a differentiation that has developed as the industry expands; and different forms of enterprise, from small, independent spaces to nodes in a network of spaces. That said, they also align their pitches along certain themes, including a sense of community and mission, common across these differences. My selection was admittedly arbitrary but proved to be productive, as the discussion of results aims to demonstrate. The five sites are *The Hive* in Hong Kong; *Impact Hub*, Bergen, Norway; *Central Working*, London; *Spaces*, Herengracht, Amsterdam; and *Spacecubed*, Perth, Australia.

Coworking: The Office Disrupted

The following discussion briefly reviews the origins and development of the coworking concept to provide context for my study. As a relatively new entrant in the marketplace, coworking spaces have been featured in popular publications, including the real estate and styles pages of *The New York Times* and the *Wall Street Journal* (e.g., Fost 2008; Williams 2013). While some discourse-oriented researchers have investigated coworking, notably Spinuzzi (2012), coworking has more often been studied by those in management, organizational behavior, marketing, computer science, and facilities planning (e.g., Balakrishnan et al. 2016; Gandini 2015; Leclercq-Vandelannoitte and Isaac 2016; Moriset 2014; Waber et al. 2014). Architecture and design firms also conduct extensive research on the state of play in workplaces, including those of existing organizations and emerging ones, like coworking enterprises. Their reports and other publications provide insights into best practices in workplace design, particularly, for my purpose, those that foster collaboration (e.g., Gensler 2018, 2019; Herman Miller 2019).

As Laing and Bacevice (2013, p. 39) argue, the movement away from fixed office space to multiple locations

> complements the plural nature of knowledge work, as work itself escapes organizational boundaries. The essential character of knowledge work in developing, communicating and sharing ideas reinforces its communal rather than solitary characteristics.

For independent workers in the twenty-first Century, mobility has meant having a choice about where to work. No longer simply taken for granted, the place of work becomes a factor in one's identity, a source, among other sources, of inspiration and motivation for work (Liegl 2014). In joining a coworking space, such workers are not looking for an office, but for people, for a community in which they can improve their work performance (Williams 2013). Coworking offers that, especially the potential for face-to-face communication and casual encounters. Laing and Bacevice (2013) point to "socially reinforced place and physical proximity as enablers of innovation and creativity" (43). Calling them "serendipity accelerators," Moriset (2014, p. 2) argues that coworking places are "powered by a specific animation intended to create links inside and outside the community of co-workers". In coworking spaces, "intensified social interaction, strengthened networking, exploration of complementarities, knowledge transfer, and learning specifically create potentials for creativity, unexpected serendipity, innovativeness and improved or new business models" (Bouncken and Reuschl 2018, p. 328).

By most accounts, coworking (a term originally hyphenated but now mostly used without the hyphen) began in San Francisco in 2005 (Fost 2008). Davies and Tollervey (2013, p. 7) call coworking a "culture rising from the underground". The original coworking spaces tended to be small, locally grown, independently owned and managed, and relatively ad hoc. Those who gathered in the space helped shape the environment and sometimes worked there for free. Coworking as an activity paralleled the open-software movement, a volunteer effort to make the world a better place through sharing. Often located in the vacated spaces of earlier economies, and in urban settings, many coworking spaces were started by entrepreneurs with an artistic bent to serve artists, designers, and other creatives who sought an inspiring aesthetic environment. The spaces tended to be eccentric in style, with high visual interest, and were only modestly remodeled from their earlier mercantile or industrial uses. The furnishings themselves were often repurposed except for a robust digital infrastructure. In these spaces, coworkers escaped the more authoritarian approach of the formal offices they had left behind and the loneliness of home.

The coworking concept has morphed, expanded in the number of enterprises and influence internationally, and gone upscale from its underground roots, although some small local sites remain. According to *Deskmag*, an online publication that tracks the growth of the shared workspace industry, by the end of 2019 almost 2.2 million people were expected to work in over 22,000 coworking spaces worldwide (Foertsch 2019). Beyond independent enterprises, coworking has fueled large-scale commercial real estate development by such major international property managers as CBRE and IWG. Architecture and design firms like Gensler and IDEO are now major players in designing coworking spaces.

In an early and frequently cited analysis of why users chose to join one or another of several coworking sites in Austin, Texas, Spinuzzi (2012) identified two overriding outcomes, which he summarized as cooperative work and parallel work. One configuration, "good partners," supports the development of collaborative networks. Independent contractors hope to connect with subcontractors to attack shared work problems and learn from each other, along the way creating "innovation networks" (Gandini 2015, p. 199). The style is casual and comfortable; coworkers benefit from interaction and feedback. They learn from each other, building trust and ensuring safety. Renters looking primarily to another outcome, "good neighbors," are less interested in networking and more in the space as a stage-set for their professional appearance. It's quieter, more like a traditional office in style. Coworkers help create a professional environment in which consultants and small business owners can meet clients.

Spinuzzi's distinction between cooperative and parallel work remains valuable, but as coworking spaces have evolved they tend to accommodate both. How they do so can be suggested by Figs. 7.1 and 7.2, photographs taken at a coworking space in Chicago. A largely open floorplan offers a variety of settings to foster diverse styles of work and leisure, privacy as well as proximity to others, and a lot of room to move around, take a break, and talk. Private office-like spaces are also available, in various sizes, in areas accessible only by keycard. All such spaces have glass doors (lockable), glass walls to a corridor, and white boards on other walls. Basic furnishings (table and chairs) and connections to technology are included, but individuals can personalize the space as they choose. Some spaces have windows with unobstructed views of Lake Michigan. In several lounge areas, those views, along with natural light, are available to all.

Figure 7.1 shows an open area on the main floor. While the couches are relatively fixed, stools and cushions are available for group seating during presentations (note the projector in the ceiling). Chairs by the

Fig. 7.1 Open area on the main floor

Fig. 7.2 Conference room on the lower floor

long tables at one end are easily moved for discussions or for individual work, with abundant outlets for plugging in the laptops and smartphones that accompany creative professionals. There's a small kitchen and bar areas.

Figure 7.2 shows a conference room on the lower level. It is next to (another) bar area but with a glass wall and door for noise abatement. The ping pong net folds away for a business meeting; the side walls are white-boards. The C is an abstraction of the logo for the Chicago Cubs, the local and much loved (and often defeated) baseball team. It brings a regional accent to what is otherwise a more corporate style. The bright orange chairs move easily. The ambiance suggests the importance of play to innovative thinking.

A Rhetorical Analysis of Five Coworking Websites

Having looked at the origins and general plan of coworking spaces, I now turn to the central focus of this chapter: an analysis of the rhetorical strategies that five coworking enterprises employ to create a virtual representation of their spaces on their websites. These representations aim to persuade customers to buy in. Consider this message on the website of WeWork:

> When we started WeWork in 2010, we wanted to build more than beautiful, shared office spaces. We wanted to build a community. A place you join as an individual, 'me', but where you become part of a greater 'we'. A place where we're redefining success measured by personal fulfillment, not just the bottom line. Community is our catalyst. (WeWork.com 2019)

A feature of this message, something prominent in each of the sites in my study, is its rhetorical persona, someone of good character who speaks for the space. This speaker, presumably the founder-entrepreneur, demonstrates adherence to a higher purpose or mission beyond the mere commercial while also displaying an attitude of empathy toward potential customers and concern for their personal fulfillment. The personal pronoun "we" first references the speaker (and the collaborative origins of the space) but then invites the customer into its plural meaning. It reinforces the notion of community, a term raised explicitly and a fundamental value of coworking. Shaped through the speaker's persona and voice, this message previews a celebratory story about a physical "place you join" where you are then transformed—your workplace revolutionized—by the people, the values, and the experience of coworking.

To analyze the strategies used in constructing such stories, I've applied the structure for persuasion identified in classical rhetorical theory (e.g., Corbett and Connors 1999). This structure is usually described in terms of three appeals designated by their Latin names: logos, ethos, and pathos. After briefly defining these terms and introducing the wordplay often involved in the names of coworking spaces, the following discussion presents the results of my research aligned by these categories.

Logos is, briefly, the rational or logical appeal. Ethos is the appeal embedded in the character of the speaker/persona as well as the values, the spirit or mission, shared by a group of people. Pathos is the appeal to our emotions, to how we experience a space or feel about something. It's often associated with aesthetics. While thinking in terms of these categories is useful for creating an argument or for analyzing how an argument has been created, the performance itself has to weave all three appeals together seamlessly to be successful. One such performance is analyzed at the end of the discussion.

The names of coworking spaces are often rhetorical gestures in themselves, clever exercises in wordplay. In a nutshell, they announce to potential customers who the founder of the space thinks they are (educated and welcoming of such play) and what awaits them in the space. Moriset (2014) draws specific attention to names in an appendix to his study of coworking, which lists some 100 spaces in cities world-wide, especially in the US, in 2013. For example, "Jigsaw Renaissance" in Seattle represents a new awakening, a place where you can put together the pieces of a puzzle in a new way; "Plug and Play" in Austin uses a familiar term for an easy way to connect and network digitally and suggests that their space provides similar affordances; "Newton's Cradle" in Albuquerque appeals to an educated, technically-savvy demographic who know about Newton and alchemy and are looking for inspiration to create new ideas; "The Hatchery," San Francisco (and other spaces with "hatch" in their name) tells start-ups they can incubate their ideas here (Moriset 2014, p. 23). Many of the names are in English, even in countries where English is not the native language (less so in France). But the English carries something of the vibe of Silicon Valley and the rise of the big US technology industry.

The names of the five spaces in my study are similarly illustrative. *The Hive* reflects collaboration (as with bees), energy, productivity, buzz. *Impact Hub*, where coworkers address sustainability and foster social impact, incorporates in its name the term "hub," a centralizing place to come together to advance such work, a diverse community. *Central Working* also evokes a coming together, as in a central train or bus station. *Spaces* as a name seems to take a different direction from centralizing to generalizing, opening up to larger uses and a broad range of customers.

The *Spaces* enterprise in my study (on the Herengracht, in Amsterdam), with its name in English, is the original location of what has become a vast network of *Spaces*-branded coworking spaces worldwide managed by IWG. *Spacecubed* evokes thoughts of an incubator, a place for new enterprises. The names in themselves predict the community and creativity to be engendered in the space.

Logos

As Figs. 7.1 and 7.2 and the discussion of the coworking space in Chicago suggest, the fundamental, rational argument for coworking is its role as an alternative physical environment for twenty-first Century work. Coworking spaces were explicitly designed to make the match between knowledge work and place, and the argument for them on their websites derives from the assumption that objects can indeed create subjects. Such spaces give independent professionals who can choose when and where to work an alternative with the right furnishing and objects to support that work.

Assuming that "work" for their potential customers means "getting creative," *Impact Hub,* for example, offers "everything you need to get creative: fast wifi, post-its, pens & markers, tea and coffee." In particular, vertical surfaces, like walls and whiteboards that you can write on (with pens and markers) and tack things on (like post-its) foster collaboration. They serve to "mak[e] thinking tangible so it can be touched, stretched, understood, and acted upon" (Doorley and Witthoft 2012, p. 157). Abundant horizontal surfaces, both tables and desks, are also available for writing individually or on a small team. Most spaces provide phone booths (without phones), nooks, or alcoves for focused work. *Central Working* has showers, a recognition that its urban customers may arrive on a bike or after a run, and want to change clothes, and is dog friendly. Access to nature and natural light are foregrounded, where available. *The Hive*, for example, features images of coworkers gathering on its deck, rare access to the outdoors in the business district of Hong Kong.

In their open areas, lounges and bars, coworking spaces encourage casual conversations and the networking aimed at accelerating innovation as well as accommodating more formal events and outreach to the community. These include routine events, like weekly breakfasts or networking meet-ups, as well as special, one-time events like talks or training programs. *Impact Hub* calls its spaces an "incubator, a project generator and an arena for events." *The Hive*'s website refers to its "best-in-class events." *Spaces* cites its "full program of professional events and hospitality services." *Central Working* calls its café in the Shoreditch section of London "a hive of collaboration and creativity." It "brings the ethos of *Central Working* to the heart of Tech City" (Davies and Tollervey 2013, p. 107).

Ethos

Central Working's reference to "ethos" is hardly an anomaly in the literature about and from coworking spaces. As the second persuasive appeal identified in classical rhetoric, ethos evokes a common bond between speaker and audience. That bond represents shared values and a shared spirit or mission and is reinforced, as we have seen, through the persona evoked in the website's text. Even as coworking becomes more institutionalized and commercialized, its origins in the sharing economy remain a point of persuasion. In language that reverberates throughout my study, Opencoworking, an international not-for-profit association of coworking founders based in the US, presents an ethical argument for the shared workspace industry. Its website lists these values that coworkers "subscribe to by being in the space":

1. Community
2. Openness
3. Collaboration
4. Accessibility
5. Sustainability

The Opencoworking (2019) website further emphasizes the commitment coworking spaces make to open sharing, with each other and with the public, and to reinforcing "the good that [coworking] can do in the world." "The power and beauty of coworking reside in its freedom to be interpreted differently" by each coworker as well as its foundation in "positivity and collaboration."

"Community," for example, is reinforced by a tendency to call coworkers *members*, not renters, even though they pay rent. (The name "WeWork" highlights this.) Membership rates emphasize flexibility, with multiple categories to meet individual choices about amount of time and type of space desired. To encourage young people and otherwise diversify the membership (diversity being one of the benefits of coworking), *The Hive*, for example, offers a special rate for those under 23. Several sites, especially in the UK, wrap their appeal in the metaphor of a "club," an exclusive (but open to nomadic members) space for a mix of leisure and work. The *Spaces* coworking site boasts the availability during regular hours of a suitably appointed "business club" where members can "meet new people without leaving the office."

Membership in a community is described as bestowing other benefits as well, for example, enhancing the reputations of coworkers, who share desired characteristics and style. Gandini (2015) calls this "reputation based on social capital" through the development of innovation networks in the space (200). *Impact Hub* specifically calls attention to the collaborative advantages in a community of "likeminded changemakers." It is home to "the innovators, the dreamers and the entrepreneurs who are creating tangible solutions to the world's most pressing issues." According to the website for *Spaces*:

> Our Spaces are inhabited by forward thinkers, innovators and game changers who are confident in achieving their goals. Whether you are a small business, entrepreneur or a corporate intrapreneur, at Spaces we help our community to expand their horizon.
>
> Our free-spirited vibe attracts an energetic community of positive and open-minded business thinkers who love to meet new people.

Another member benefit, similar to the benefits offered by private clubs which have reciprocal privileges at other clubs, is privileged access to partner organizations. The partners may offer special discounts at hotels and restaurants, priority service at a range of attractions, tickets for museums and shows, special rates on publications and printing service, connections to professional business organizations and entrepreneurial associations, rental bikes (in the Netherlands), and the like. Coworking spaces that are part of a network also offer the option to work at any club when a member of one of them.

In addition, to help members connect virtually between their visits, and participate in the coworking ethos when they are not actually in the space, some coworking spaces publish magazines about their activities available online, host blogs created by members, and offer links to articles of interest published in the media. In my study, all of these options were available as well to potential members as a marketing device. A special section of the *Impact Hub* website, for example, labeled "Impact Stories," features member blogs and news so members can "read about learnings from peers on their impact journeys." *Central Working* provides an extensive bibliography about coworking in general and about *Central Working* in particular. *The Hive* emphasizes that "our Hivers App, and our community engagement empowers our members with the network effect. Helping them build deep, lasting connections across *the Hive* membership base, whatever their industry, role or location." This mention of an app references another benefit provided by some spaces: a password-protected platform for member communication separate from the open-access website.

As the number of coworking spaces has grown, some are differentiating themselves by establishing an ethical bond with a particular demographic. These include, for example, coworking spaces for veterans, or writers, or leaders of small non-profit organizations, or graphic artists. While none of the websites in my study targets only women as customers, several incorporate women in their appeals, reaching out to a group often underserved in other high-tech organizations. An early proponent of coworking—and accessibility—argues that spaces focused on women entrepreneurs are "exploding" (Baciagalupo 2017). Some are exclusive to women, as noted in their name, for example, *CoworkHERS* in Portland, Maine. *Loffice*, a coworking site in Budapest, targets a demographic they call, in a lovely twist on English, "newborn parents." With the informal name "coworkid," the space aims to connect new parents, men and women who are professionals interested in flexible work, with entrepreneurs looking for such workers. Child care is incorporated in the mix (Davies and Tollervey 2013, p. 120). *The Hive* in Hong Kong talks about its appeal to independent creatives it calls "mumpreneurs" (Davies and Tollervey 2013, p. 46). *Spacecubed* in Perth, Australia, claims on its website that it serves women by partnering with an organization that "empowers and helps women learn coding by organising free programming workshops and meetups … to increase the diversity in the tech community, and to spark collaboration, creativity, and expand networks."

Both *Impact Hub* and *Spacecubed* differentiate themselves by appealing to a demographic specifically focused on sustainability, broadly understood as a social as well as an ecological movement. Sustainability is often mentioned as a coworking value, demonstrated in part by the many spaces that emerged in buildings abandoned by earlier economies. Indeed, Jane Jacobs (1961), the urban economist who extolls the value of neighborhoods and organic growth, argues that old ideas can exist in new buildings, but that new ideas come best from old buildings. *Impact Hub* and *Spacecubed* had such origins; sustainability underpins their brand.

Impact Hub, in Bergen, Norway, occupies two wooden warehouses dating from 1702 in a harbor area prominent in the days of the Hanseatic League and currently a UNESCO historic site. Limited in funds for renovating the space, the founder invited local art and design students to help, a source of free ideas and a way to inform young creatives about the space. Most of the original furniture was "vintage, bespoke or upcycled" to explicitly save money and enhance sustainability (Davies and Tollervey 2013, p. 55). Originally an independent enterprise called *The Hub*, it has now expanded as part of a network of 101 "inspiring locations" focused on social innovation. Their embrace of the value of openness is shown in community programs that aim to "make a positive impact in the world." This includes reducing air pollution and improving care for the elderly. Their members value "inspiring, connecting, and enabling citizens, entrepreneurs and organisations—to work together in collaborative environments and to jointly create resilient entrepreneurial ecosystems" (Davies and Tollervey 2013, p. 57).

Similarly, *Spacecubed* in Perth, Australia, emphasizes sustainability and social innovation as prominent values shared by its coworkers. Housed in a former Reserve Bank of Australia building, the original coworking space was built using 75 percent recycled materials "to encourage sustainability in Perth" (Davies and Tollervey 2013, p. 149). It was also "shaped by the community of people who use it and has evolved organically over time." That community includes social and environmental entrepreneurs, technology and creative startups, and government and corporate innovation teams. The brand statement on their 2019 website reads "empowering positive change through community." Members can also connect with an industry-specific hub and a makerspace. Organizers of *Spacecubed* offer programs and grants to support their "passionate, driven community of collaborators fostering creativity and engagement." The "Impact" button on *Spacecubed*'s home page links to statements about their program of mentoring and their grants aimed at "social impact and prioritising gender diversity in the workplace, inclusion and empowerment through entrepreneurship." The three major themes are (1) "Enterprise education and experiential learning for youth"; (2) "Supporting regional innovation and enabling peer learning across regional communities"; and (3) "entrepreneurship research."

Pathos

Reference to a "passionate, driven community of collaborators" evokes the third appeal of classical rhetoric, the appeal to emotions. Beyond finding the right office-like affordances to get their work done, and in a setting in which they'll collaborate with the right people who share their values and will enhance their innovative thinking, potential members will find in the space the right aesthetics, the right *feel.* The space will give them the right experience. It will make their work enjoyable and make them happy. Given the consumerist society of the twenty-first Century, and a trend toward the aestheticizing of work, it's important that people feel good in the space. Gensler (2018), for example, asserts that "The connection between a great experience and business performance is well documented." This reputation of coworking is what the developers of federally funded opportunity zones in declining industrial cities of the US, for example, rely on to keep young professionals who would otherwise abandon them for San Francisco or Boston near home.

The founder of *Spaces* asked its designer in 2008 to create "spaces that are fun, inspiring and sociable to work in … a personalized and homely environment to encourage interaction and collaboration" (Davies and Tollervey 2013, p. 113). Under the heading "What we deliver," the founder of the *Hive* notes on its website, "By delivering an exceptional Hive Experience, [with the capital letter E] we strive to ensure that every one of our members has a happy and successful day, every day." Valuing openness and warmth, he boasts that "our team is passionate about providing an uplifting workplace experience."

Like the founder of *Spaces,* coworking entrepreneurs are increasingly turning to professional space planners and designers to help them create attractive workplace experiences. What they learn from such designers, and the process of design thinking itself, is often reflected in their pitches. Most important, design thinking is human-centered. It begins in empathy, that is, understanding and sharing the feelings of others. It depends on close observation of potential customers, gaining an empirical knowledge of what they need, even when potential customers can't articulate or imagine what they might want that a coworking space could provide. Coworking entrepreneurs need to create the desire in their pitches before their potential customers can see that they need the space, before they can imagine themselves in the space. That creation, I argue, is a rhetorical enterprise of its own.

In Performance: The Appeals Combined

To demonstrate how these rational, ethical, and emotional appeals can be effectively integrated in a persuasive story, told through an empathetical rhetorical persona, I've included below the full text of "*Central Working*, In our own Words" from the space's website. The text is also a script, linked to a 2+minute Vimeo video featuring James Layfield, founder of *Central Working*, as he relaxes, in casual clothes, while seated on a couch in the space. In the video, Layfield the person demonstrates the good character of the founder-entrepreneur described earlier as an important element in each website in the study. The script as posted on the site varies somewhat awkwardly between description and first-person statements as it establishes the story's context and argument. It does, however, consistently address the potential customer as "you." Two headings, "The story of why" and "Our values," and four quoted testimonials about the space break up the text and reinforce the argument that *Central Working* meets three big challenges (the third cast as a value) to new entrepreneurs: space, support, and a magical experience of community. To incorporate my commentary, I've divided the text into segments here, although it runs uninterrupted on the site.

> **The story of why**
> Central Working was started to address challenges that James Layfield, founder, believes all new business owners are affected by. The first was the space. Why sign leases for three, four, or even five years when you have no way of knowing how big or small your business will be in that time? Wouldn't you prefer a space with soul, and a place you can envisage yourself going to work everyday? Somewhere you'll be more likely to connect with the talent that you want to attract.

The text begins by introducing Layfield as an entrepreneur who knows the challenges that entrepreneurs face. It sets up ("first") a list of such challenges and poses rhetorical questions directly to you, the potential customer, questions that demonstrate his knowledge of what entrepreneurs need. The first question introduces an important logical appeal of coworking: variable lease arrangements. The last question (although without a question mark) speaks to the ethical appeal: you'll meet the right people ("talent") to join you in your enterprise. The second question engages the emotional appeal: a space "with soul" where you'll feel right. In asking these questions the speaker [Layfield in the video] demonstrates empathy while allowing the potential customer to give the (expected) answers. They'll convince themselves, a much more powerful approach to persuasion then simply telling them.

> The second was support. It's really difficult to be an entrepreneur, running your own business. There will be difficult times or issues that you might not feel you can speak to your team about, these problems then get bottled up and cause you unnecessary stress.

[First testimonial] "Central Working offers incredible flexibility with no leases to worry about. We also give you a genuine support network."

That's why Central Working offers incredible flexibility with no leases to worry about. We also give you a genuine support network; other people like you, running businesses, having problems, helping each other by sharing their experience and knowledge.

The second challenge, announced earlier, is the need for support. The option of flexibility in leases is repeated. Support is introduced. Empathy for those "running your own business" is reconfirmed. The story is now directly told by Layfield: "We … give you a support network." The text references a common communication problem: not being able to talk with your team about "difficult times or issues" so these issues get "bottled up" and cause you stress. Not having to sign a lease is one way to relieve stress. The "support network" is even more important. Evoking the "genuine support network" further reinforces the ethical appeal of membership: a collaborative network for communication

Our values

Lots of people talk about 'community' and 'networking', but they just mean something random that relies on serendipity. At Central Working when we talk about reinvigorating community, we mean something much more reliable than that.

[Second testimonial] "When you walk into a Central Working location, you can feel that these people care about you."

You spend most of your time in your office, so we've created a workplace that gives you a real and supportive community. It isn't random, and is made up of people that really want to look after you and care for you, making you want to come into work each day. When you walk into a Central Working location, you can feel that these people care about you - not just our team, but the membership as a whole - it's a real community, for you.

[Third testimonial] "Our team don't have computers to sit behind; they will have a conversation with you. know your name and about your company, they care about you and what you do."

"Our values" as a heading is not logically parallel with "The story of why" and comes in mid-text, which continues to discuss the second challenge (support). But the heading does reinforce the ethical appeal of a value-driven enterprise. As we've seen in this chapter, "community" and "networking," even "serendipity," are key marketing terms for coworking spaces. Within that context, Layfield refers to something special, setting up the discussion that follows, the differentiator. The second testimonial, from a speaker/member about the staff, and the third, spoken presumably by Layfield, reinforce the picture of a caring place, an empathetic community.

> It's pretty common to see someone walking around with their nose buried in their phone, and to us, that isn't how business is done. The magic happens when you're sat across a table, looking another person in the eye, talking to them with enthusiasm; that's why our second value is about cherishing human connection. Email, Facebook, even instant messenger doesn't offer that; that's why we put you in the room with the right people.
>
> [Fourth testimonial] "The word love isn't used a huge amount in business, but we think it's important."
>
> The way that those human connections help you is our third value: creating magical moments, with love, care and attention. The word love isn't used a huge amount in business, but we think it's important. Your workspace is where you spend most of your time, so if you don't feel like there's some truly inspirational magic in the air, what is the point? With us, you'll be able to create moments that encourage your business to thrive.
>
> Our members tell us there's something amazing about our spaces, and we believe it's the amount of effort and love that we put in. We can tell you our story, but the only way to really 'get it' is to come in and feel the difference for yourself.

This segment of the text/talk rises fully to the emotional appeal: "creating magical moments, with love, care and attention." The image of people with noses buried in their smart phones contrasts with the picture of staff and coworkers at *Central Working* "cherishing human connection." People at *Central Working* talk to each other. Proximity and face-to-face communication matter, even more than social media and messaging apps. To achieve enthusiastic (and presumably productive and pleasurable) communication, “we put you in the room with the right people.”

The final testimonial introduces the concept of love, the ultimate positive emotion but a term rarely used in business. It should be, the speaker argues, because you, the entrepreneur and potential member, spend most of your time in your workspace. It’s unreasonable to spend that time somewhere that lacks “truly inspirational magic in the air.” The message: you’ll find it here. The repetition of the sentence beginning “The word love isn’t used….” reiterates that argument. Love and effort create spaces that “our members” tell us are “something amazing.” Place makes magic. The pitch ends with an invitation to come to the space and “feel the difference.” Join the experience. Join the place.

Conclusion

“The Story of Central Working” pulls together with gusto key elements of the larger coworking story presented in the five websites which are the focus of this chapter. Hardly elegant or even grammatically correct, Layfield’s text still creates a strong and persuasive image of coworking as a values-driven enterprise that will enhance its members’ productivity and pleasure as they work. It demonstrates the power of a rhetorical persona who speaks for the enterprise (perhaps more so in the video) and employs well-tested strategies of persuasion—logical, ethical, and emotional—in building an argument in virtual space for the spatial experience a customer will find on the ground.

That said, in looking back on each of these websites as I write in 2020, I seem to be looking at another world. In particular, assumptions about community, the social creation of knowledge through face-to-face communication, the collaborative origins of innovation, and the importance of place—these seem, like the coworking spaces themselves, relics of a far distant past. It’s hard to know what form knowledge work, now mostly digital, will take when the world reopens.

Whatever form work takes, however, it will have to take place, someplace, and thus the agency of place will continue to be an important research concern. This study of coworking websites has been something of an aside from such research. But it has uncovered an interesting data base in itself and illustrates the productivity of a mixed-methods approach in illuminating this data. Of the themes being addressed in this volume, such *triangulation* comes to the forefront in my research. The study is also tied to an interesting new concept for a workplace, making this business and professional *background* relevant. These workplaces were real and thus research on them is, I'd argue, *authentic* even if their virtual representations, the object of my study, are artifices created through rhetorical strategies. The fourth theme, *saturation,* was not a concern. My study in the end aimed to be suggestive, to offer new ways to find and analyze data rather than to close an argument around a determined sufficiency of data found.

In conclusion, let me suggest two ways to extend this mixed-methods approach as new forms of knowledge work prevail beyond the particular configuration of a workplace represented by coworking spaces.

First, once I had identified these stories of coworking as a rhetorical genre, I realized that, in fact, they were also exemplars of the kind of communication entrepreneurs pitching any innovative idea, service, or product must create. The activities and the writing needed to create an organization and market that organization often differ from such practices in existing organizations (e.g., Spartz and Weber 2015). Among other differences, this requires storytelling, narratives that envision a scene in the future in which customers can imagine themselves using, to great benefit, the app or other product the entrepreneur has created for them, whether the potential customers know they need it or not. These coworking websites are good examples of entrepreneurial storytelling, and research on them can inform other entrepreneurs as they write their own organizations into being.

Second, as I applied theory and method from classical rhetoric to these pitches, I was also reminded about the powerful role rhetorical tropes, particularly metaphor and personification, play in enhancing creativity and communication. This may seem obvious but is worth restating. Phrases like "join a place," "inspiring location," "collaborative environment," "make thinking tangible," "a place with soul," "personalized and homely environment," are among many quoted in the chapter that attribute the characteristics and abilities of humans in real places to the rhetorical place being evoked. Communicating a new idea or a new place through metaphor—giving human characteristics to an object—can have subtle, persuasive appeal. I've only touched on metaphoric implications in this study, as in the list of names for coworking spaces, but the data warrant another look with that in mind.

For the larger picture of research on business and professional discourse, I hope this study has at least sketched an inviting area of interest at the intersection of questions about the agency of text, which is the province of classical rhetoric, and the agency of place, which is the concern of material culture studies and design thinking.

References

Andrews, D. (2016). The physical environment for communication in 21st century workspaces: A research model. In G. M. Alessi & G. Jacobs (Eds.), *The ins and outs of business and professional discourse research* (pp. 37–62). London: Palgrave Macmillan.

Andrews, D. (2017). A space for place in business communication research. *International Journal of Business Communication, 54*, 325–336.

Andrews, D. (2018). Investigating the workspaces of science. In K. R. Moore & D. P. Richards (Eds.), *Posthuman praxis in technical communication* (pp. 255–280). New York: Routledge.

Baciagalupo, T. (2017). Open coworking. Building the movement together. *2017 impact report.* Retrieved from https://www.slideshare.net/slideshow/embed_code/key/421FjIFofuobOD.

Balakrishnan, B. K. P. D., Muthaly, S., & Leenders, M. (2016). Insights from coworking spaces as unique service organizations: The role of physical and social elements. In L. Petruzzellis & R. S. Winer (Eds.), *Rediscovering the essentiality of marketing* (Developments in marketing science: Proceedings of the academy of marketing science). Springer.

Bouncken, R., & Reuschl, A. J. (2018). Coworking-spaces: How a phenomenon of the sharing economy builds a novel trend for the workplace and for entrepreneurship. *Review of Management Science, 12*, 317–334.

Central Working, London. Retrieved from https://centralworking.com/locations/shoreditch.

Corbett, E. P. J., & Connors, R. J. (1999). *Classical rhetoric for the modern student* (4th ed.). New York: Oxford University Press.

Davies, A., & Tollervey, K. (2013). *The style of coworking: Contemporary shared workspaces*. Munich: Prestel.

Doorley, S., & Witthoft, S. (2012). *Make space: How to set the stage for creative collaboration*. Hoboken, NJ: John Wiley & Sons.

Foertsch, C. (2019). 2019 State of coworking: Over 2 million coworking space members expected. Deskmag. Retrieved from http://www.deskmag.com/en/2019-state-of-coworking-spaces-2-million-members-growth-crisis-market-report-survey-study.

Fost, D. (2008, February 20). They're working on their own, just side by side. *The New York Times*. Retrieved from https://www.nytimes.com/2008/02/20/business/businessspecial2/20cowork.html?_r=1&ex=1361250000&en=dbd589ebb73df147&ei=5090&partner=rssuserland&emc=rss&oref=slogin.

Gandini, A. (2015). The rise of coworking spaces: A literature review. *Ephemera: Theory and Politics in Organization, 15*, 193–205.

Gensler. (2018). Co-working: What's right for your brand? Retrieved from https://www.gensler.com/research-insight/publications/dialogue/31/coworking-whats-right-for-your-brand?utm_source=webdownload-contacts_2018july24&utm_medium=email&utm_campaign=dialogue-31.

Gensler. (2019). *2019 US workplace survey/key findings*. Retrieved from www.gensler.com/research-insight/workplace-surveys/us.

Herman Miller. (2019). Living office. Placemaking. Retrieved from https://www.hermanmiller.com/solutions/living-office/placemaking/.

Impact Hub Bergen. Retrieved from https://bergen.impacthub.net/what-is-impact-hub/.

Jacobs, J. (1961). *The death and life of great American cities*. New York: Random House.

Laing, A., & Bacevice, P. A. (2013). Using design to drive organizational performance and innovation in the corporate workplace: Implications for interprofessional environments. *Journal of Interprofessional Care, 27*(Supp 2), 37–45. https://doi.org/10.3109/13561820.2013.792043.

Leclercq-Vandelannoitte, A., & Isaac, H. (2016). The new office: How coworking changes the work concept. *Journal of Business Strategy, 37*, 3–9.

Liegl, M. (2014). Nomadicity and the care of place—On the aesthetic and affective organization of space in freelance creative work. *Computer Supported Cooperative Work, 23*, 163–183.

Miller, D. (2008). *The comfort of things*. London: Polity.
Miller, D. (2010). *Stuff.* Cambridge, UK and Malden MA: Polity.
Moriset, B. (2014). *Building new places of the creative economy: Coworking spaces.* Presented at the 2nd Geography of Innovation International Conference, Utrecht University, Utrecht, the Netherlands.
Overmyer, T., & Carlson, E. B. (2019). Literature review: Design thinking and place. *Journal of Business and Technical Communication, 33*, 431–436.
Spacecubed. Perth, Australia. Retrieved from https://www.spacecubed.com/spaces.
Spaces, Herengracht, Amsterdam. Retrieved from https://www.spacesworks.com/amsterdam/herengracht/.
Spartz, J. M., & Weber, R. P. (2015). Writing entrepreneurs: A survey of attitudes, habits, skills, and genres. *Journal of Business and Technical Communication, 29*, 428–455.
Spinuzzi, C. (2012). Working alone together: Coworking as emergent collaborative activity. *Journal of Business and Technical Communication, 26*, 399–441.
The Hive Hong Kong. Retrieved from https://thehive.com.hk/.
Values. (2019). Open Coworking. Building the movement together. Retrieved from http://opencoworking.org/news/about/values/.
Waber, B., Magnolfi, J., & Lindsay, G. (2014, October). Workspaces that move people. *Harvard Business Review*, 69–77. Retrieved from https://hbr.org/2014/10/workspaces-that-move-people?referral=03758&cm_vc=rr_item_page.top_right.
WeWork's IPO: Risky Business. (2019, August 17). *The Economist*, 50.
Williams, A. (2013, May 5). Working alone, together. *The New York Times, 5*(May), 1–16.

Index[1]

[1] Note: Page numbers followed by 'n' refer to notes.

G. Jacobs, S. Decock (eds.), *Good Data in Business and Professional Discourse Research and Teaching*, Communicating in Professions and Organizations,
https://doi.org/10.1007/978-3-030-61757-8

GPSR Compliance
The European Union's (EU) General Product Safety Regulation (GPSR) is a set of rules that requires consumer products to be safe and our obligations to ensure this.

If you have any concerns about our products, you can contact us on

ProductSafety@springernature.com

In case Publisher is established outside the EU, the EU authorized representative is:

Springer Nature Customer Service Center GmbH
Europaplatz 3
69115 Heidelberg, Germany

www.ingramcontent.com/pod-product-compliance
Lightning Source LLC
Chambersburg PA
CBHW020727050526
44254CB00090B/4
* 9 7 8 3 0 3 0 6 1 7 5 6 1 *